THE SMART PASTA COOKBOOK

Fall River Press
122 Fifth Avenue
New York, NY 10011

ISBN: 978-1-4351-2939-9

Printed and bound in China

10 9 8 7 6 5 4 3 2 1

Cover *Casarecci with spring greens and goat's cheese, page 232*
Photographer *Brett Stevens* Stylist *Yael Grinham*

THE SMART PASTA COOKBOOK

Fall River Press

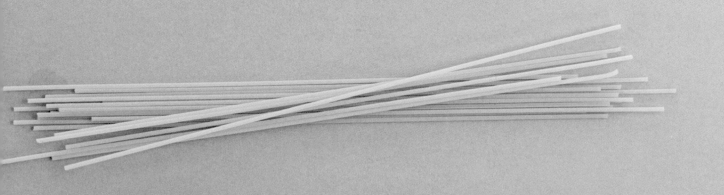

contents

angel hair

Also known as capelli d'angelo, angel hair is sold as small, circular nests of very fine, delicate pasta strands; its cooking time is minimal because it's so thin.

angel hair frittata

4oz angel hair pasta
1 tablespoon vegetable oil
1 small leek (7oz), chopped coarsely
2 cloves garlic, crushed
¼ cup (1oz) finely grated Parmesan cheese
7oz feta cheese, crumbled
2oz spinach leaves, chopped coarsely
½ cup (4oz) sour cream
¼ teaspoon ground nutmeg
6 eggs, beaten lightly

1 Cook pasta in large saucepan of boiling water until tender; drain.
2 Meanwhile, heat oil in 8in frying pan; cook leek and garlic, stirring, until leek softens.
3 Combine pasta and leek mixture in large bowl with Parmesan and half the feta, spinach, sour cream, nutmeg and egg. Pour mixture into same frying pan; cook, covered, over low heat 10 minutes.
4 Preheat grill.
5 Remove cover from pan; grill about 5 minutes or until frittata sets and top browns lightly. Stand in pan 5 minutes. Top with remaining feta before serving with a mixed leaf salad, if you like.

prep & cook time 30 minutes **serves** 4
nutritional count per serving 38.1g total fat (19.6g saturated fat); 524 cal; 19.7g carbohydrate; 25.3g protein; 2.4g fiber

Angel hair pasta, the finest of pastas, produces the best results in this frittata because it lends a smooth-textured consistency.

angel hair pasta with smoked salmon & asparagus

13oz angel hair pasta
¼ cup (60ml) olive oil
9oz asparagus, trimmed, chopped coarsely
5oz smoked salmon, sliced thinly
2 tablespoons rinsed, drained baby capers
⅓ cup finely chopped fresh chives
3oz baby rocket leaves
1 lemon, cut into wedges

1 Cook pasta in large saucepan of boiling water until tender; drain. Return pasta to pan.
2 Meanwhile, heat oil in small frying pan; cook asparagus, stirring, until tender.
3 Add asparagus, salmon, capers, chives and rocket to pasta; toss to combine. Serve pasta with lemon wedges.

prep & cook time 15 minutes **serves** 4
nutritional count per serving 16.6g total fat (2.5g saturated fat); 509 cal; 66g carbohydrate; 20.9g protein; 4.7g fiber

angel hair pasta with rocket, tomato and feta

13oz angel hair pasta
7oz feta cheese, crumbled
¼ cup (60ml) olive oil
2 fresh small red thai chilies, chopped finely
2 tablespoons coarsely shredded fresh basil
¼ cup coarsely chopped fresh flat-leaf parsley
3 cloves garlic, crushed
3 medium tomatoes (1lb 4oz), seeded,
   sliced thinly
9oz rocket, chopped coarsely

1 Cook pasta in large saucepan of boiling water until tender; drain.
2 Meanwhile, place cheese in large bowl with oil, chili, herbs, garlic, tomato and rocket; toss to combine. Add pasta; toss gently.

prep & cook time 20 minutes **serves** 4
nutritional count per serving 26.9g total fat (9.8g saturated fat); 608 cal; 66.8g carbohydrate; 21.8g protein; 5.3g fiber

tuna, olive and rocket pasta

9oz angel hair pasta

15oz can tuna chunks in olive oil, drained, flaked

⅓ cup (2oz) seeded kalamata olives,
    quartered lengthways

9oz cherry tomatoes, halved

⅓ cup (2oz) roasted pine nuts

4oz baby rocket leaves

lemon mustard dressing

2 tablespoons olive oil

1 tablespoon finely grated lemon rind

¼ cup (60ml) lemon juice

1 clove garlic, crushed

1 tablespoon Dijon mustard

1 Make lemon mustard dressing.

2 Cook pasta in large saucepan of boiling water until tender; drain.

3 Place pasta in large bowl with tuna, olives, tomato, nuts and rocket. Drizzle dressing over pasta mixture; toss gently.

lemon mustard dressing Combine ingredients in screw-top jar; shake well.

prep & cook time 30 minutes **serves** 4

nutritional count per serving 30.9g total fat (3.9g saturated fat); 606 cal; 48.9g carbohydrate; 31g protein; 4.6g fiber

shrimp pad thai

1lb 5oz uncooked medium jumbo shrimp
½in piece fresh ginger, grated
2 cloves garlic, crushed
1 fresh small red thai chili, sliced thinly
1½ tablespoons grated palm sugar
¼ cup (60ml) soy sauce
2 tablespoons sweet chili sauce
1 tablespoon fish sauce
1½ tablespoons tomato paste
9oz angel hair pasta
1 tablespoon sesame oil
6 green onions, sliced thinly
2 cups (6oz) bean sprouts
½ cup loosely packed fresh coriander leaves

1 Shell and devein shrimp, leaving tails intact. Place shrimp in large bowl with ginger, garlic and chili; toss gently. Place sugar, sauces and paste in screw-top jar; shake well.
2 Cook pasta in large saucepan of boiling water until tender; drain.
3 Meanwhile, heat oil in wok; stir-fry shrimp mixture, in batches, until shrimp just change color. Return shrimp to wok, add sauce mixture; stir-fry 1 minute or until heated through. Remove from heat; add onion, bean sprouts, coriander and pasta, toss gently.

prep & cook time 25 minutes **serves** 4
nutritional count per serving 6.2g total fat (0.9g saturated fat); 382 cal; 52.6g carbohydrate; 25.8g protein; 4.9g fiber

Commercial laksa pastes vary dramatically in their heat intensity so try using less of the laksa paste you've purchased until you can determine how hot it makes the final dish.

angel hair seafood laksa

1lb 2oz uncooked medium jumbo shrimp
1 tablespoon laksa paste
2 cups (500ml) vegetable stock
2 cups (500ml) water
400ml coconut cream
11oz firm white fish fillets, chopped coarsely
9oz angel hair pasta
11oz baby bok choy, chopped coarsely
4 green onions, sliced thinly
¼ cup loosely packed fresh coriander leaves

1 Shell and devein shrimp, leaving tails intact.
2 Cook paste in heated large saucepan, stirring, until fragrant. Stir in shrimp, stock, the water, coconut cream and fish; bring to the boil. Reduce heat; simmer, uncovered, until shrimp change color and fish is just cooked.
3 Meanwhile, cook pasta in large saucepan of boiling water until tender; drain.
4 While pasta is cooking, stir bok choy, onion and coriander into laksa mixture; cook, uncovered, until bok choy is just wilted.
5 Divide pasta among bowls; top with laksa mixture.

prep & cook time 25 minutes **serves** 4
nutritional count per serving 24.2g total fat
(19.1g saturated fat); 582 cal; 48.6g carbohydrate;
39.5g protein; 5.1g fiber

spicy rocket pasta

2 tablespoons olive oil
1 teaspoon dried chili flakes
2 cloves garlic, crushed
½ teaspoon cracked black pepper
¼ cup (60ml) lemon juice
13oz angel hair pasta
3oz rocket leaves
2 medium tomatoes (11oz), seeded,
    chopped coarsely
⅔ cup firmly packed fresh basil leaves

1 Heat oil in large frying pan; cook chili and garlic, stirring, until fragrant. Add pepper and juice; stir until hot.
2 Meanwhile, cook pasta in large saucepan of boiling water until tender; drain.
3 Combine chili mixture and pasta in large bowl with rocket, tomato and basil.

prep & cook time 20 minutes **serves** 4
nutritional count per serving 10.4g total fat (1.5g saturated fat); 420 cal; 66.4g carbohydrate; 12.1g protein; 4.8g fiber

hot & sour shrimp pasta

2lbs 4oz cooked medium jumbo shrimp
9oz angel hair pasta
1 lime
1 lemon
1 medium red pepper (7oz), sliced thinly
1 medium yellow pepper (7oz), sliced thinly
1 medium red onion (6oz), sliced thinly
¼ cup (60ml) olive oil
¼ cup (60ml) rice vinegar
1 tablespoon sambal oelek
1 tablespoon fish sauce
2 tablespoons grated palm sugar
1 cup firmly packed fresh coriander leaves

1 Shell and devein shrimp, leaving tails intact.
2 Cook pasta in large saucepan of boiling water until tender; drain.
3 Meanwhile, halve lime and lemon lengthways; thinly slice 1 unpeeled half of each, place in large bowl. Squeeze juice from remaining halves into bowl; add shrimp, pasta and remaining ingredients, toss gently. Cover; refrigerate 1 hour before serving.

prep & cook time 35 minutes (+ refrigeration) **serves** 4
nutritional count per serving 15.4g total fat
(2.2g saturated fat); 516 cal; 56g carbohydrate;
35.6g protein; 4.6g fiber

angel hair pasta, chicken and rocket

9oz angel hair pasta
1 tablespoon olive oil
1 medium onion (5oz), chopped finely
1lb 11oz ground chicken
1 tablespoon tomato paste
25oz bottled tomato sauce
2 teaspoons dried basil
3oz rocket
2 tablespoons finely grated Parmesan cheese
9oz coarsely grated mozzarella cheese

1 Cook pasta in large saucepan of boiling water until tender; drain.
2 Meanwhile, heat oil in large saucepan; cook onion, stirring, until just softened. Add chicken; cook, stirring, 4 minutes. Add paste; cook, stirring, until chicken is cooked through. Add sauce; cook, stirring, 5 minutes. Remove from heat; stir in basil.
3 Preheat grill. Place half of the pasta in oiled 8-cup ovenproof dish. Top with half of the chicken mixture, rocket and Parmesan; repeat with remaining pasta and chicken mixture. Top with mozzarella; place under grill about 2 minutes or until mozzarella melts.

prep & cook time 30 minutes **serves** 4
nutritional count per serving 29.4g total fat (12.7g saturated fat); 796 cal; 62.2g carbohydrate; 67g protein; 6.2g fiber

Stir in ⅓ cup coarsely chopped fresh basil leaves just before serving, if you like. Baby capers could also be added to this recipe.

tuna and chili pasta

13oz angel hair pasta
15oz can tuna in oil
4 cloves garlic, sliced thinly
1 teaspoon dried chili flakes
⅓ cup (80ml) dry white wine
14oz can chopped tomatoes
1 tablespoon lemon juice

1 Cook pasta in large saucepan of boiling water until tender; drain, reserving ¼ cup cooking liquid. Rinse pasta under cold water, drain.
2 Meanwhile, drain tuna, reserving 2 tablespoons of the oil. Heat oil in medium frying pan, add garlic; cook, stirring, until fragrant. Add chili and wine; cook, uncovered, until wine is almost evaporated. Add undrained tomatoes, tuna and reserved cooking liquid; simmer until liquid has reduced slightly. Remove from heat; stir in juice. Combine pasta and sauce in large bowl.

prep & cook time 15 minutes **serves** 4
nutritional count per serving 22.3g total fat (3.2g saturated fat); 626 cal; 67.5g carbohydrate; 32.5g protein; 4.8g fiber

Stir in some fresh mint leaves and replace the ricotta cheese with feta cheese.

lemon, pea and ricotta pasta

13oz angel hair pasta
2 cups (9oz) frozen peas
2 tablespoons olive oil
2 cloves garlic, sliced thinly
2 teaspoons finely grated lemon rind
½ cup (125ml) lemon juice
¾ cup (6oz) firm ricotta cheese, crumbled

1 Cook pasta in large saucepan of boiling water until tender; add peas during last minute of pasta cooking time. Drain, reserving ¼ cup cooking liquid. Rinse pasta and peas under cold water; drain.
2 Meanwhile, heat oil in small frying pan; cook garlic, stirring, until fragrant.
3 Combine pasta and peas in large bowl with reserved cooking liquid, garlic mixture, rind and juice; stir in cheese.

prep & cook time 15 minutes **serves** 4
nutritional count per serving 15.6g total fat (4.7g saturated fat); 508 cal; 69g carbohydrate; 19g protein; 6.9g fiber

fettuccine

Fettuccine, a long, flat, ribbon pasta made of egg and flour, is known as 'little ribbons' in Italian. It is similar to tagliatelle.

fettuccine alle vongole

2 tablespoons olive oil
3 cloves garlic, crushed
1 fresh long red chili, chopped finely
1 tablespoon rinsed, drained baby capers
¾ cup (180ml) dry white wine
¾ cup (180ml) fish stock
2 tablespoons lemon juice
2lbs 4oz clams
13oz fettuccine pasta
½ cup coarsely chopped fresh flat-leaf parsley
¼ cup coarsely chopped fresh chives

1 Heat oil in large saucepan; cook garlic and chili, stirring, 1 minute. Add capers, wine, stock and juice; bring to the boil. Add clams; cook, covered, about 5 minutes or until clams open (discard any that do not).
2 Meanwhile, cook pasta in large saucepan of boiling water until tender; drain.
3 Add pasta and herbs to clam mixture; toss gently.

prep & cook time 30 minutes **serves** 4
nutritional count per serving 10.5g total fat (1.6g saturated fat); 479 cal; 65.9g carbohydrate; 20.2g protein; 4g fiber

A classic Italian pasta, alle vongole (Italian for 'clams') is usually made with tiny baby clams, but you can use any clams you like for this recipe.

fettuccine carbonara

1lb 2oz fettuccine pasta
14oz bacon, sliced thinly
4oz button mushrooms, sliced thinly
1¼ cups (300ml) cream
4 eggs, beaten lightly
1 cup (3oz) coarsely grated Parmesan cheese

1 Cook pasta in large saucepan of boiling water until tender; drain. Return pasta to pan; cover to keep warm.
2 Meanwhile, cook bacon in large frying pan, stirring, until crisp. Add mushrooms; cook, stirring, until tender. Add cream; stir until heated through.
3 Working quickly, gently combine bacon mixture, hot pasta and combined egg and cheese. Serve topped with fresh oregano leaves, if you like.

prep & cook time 20 minutes **serves** 4
nutritional count per serving 57.6g total fat
(31.9g saturated fat); 815 cal; 33.5g carbohydrate;
40.4g protein; 2.9g fiber

fettuccine alfredo

13oz fettuccine pasta
3oz butter, chopped coarsely
⅔ cup (160ml) cream
1 cup (3oz) finely grated Parmesan cheese
2 tablespoons finely chopped fresh flat-leaf parsley

1 Cook pasta in large saucepan of boiling water until tender; drain. Return pasta to pan; cover to keep warm.
2 Meanwhile, stir butter and cream in medium saucepan over low heat until butter melts and combines well with the cream; remove from heat. Add cheese; stir until sauce is blended and smooth.
3 Pour sauce over hot pasta, toss well; sprinkle with parsley to serve.

prep & cook time 20 minutes **serves** 4
nutritional count per serving 43.3g total fat
(27.9g saturated fat); 731 cal; 65.3g carbohydrate;
19.1g protein; 3.2g fiber

pagli e fieno

5oz plain fettuccine pasta
5oz spinach-flavored fettuccine pasta
2 teaspoons olive oil
5 green onions, sliced thinly
2 cloves garlic, crushed
1lb 2oz button mushrooms, sliced thickly
1 tablespoon dry white wine
1¼ cups (300ml) cream
¼ cup coarsely chopped fresh flat-leaf parsley

1 Cook both pastas in large saucepan of boiling water until tender; drain.
2 Meanwhile, heat oil in medium saucepan; cook onion and garlic, stirring, until onion softens. Add mushrooms; cook, stirring, until just browned. Add wine and cream; bring to the boil. Reduce heat; simmer, uncovered, about 5 minutes or until sauce thickens slightly. Stir in parsley.
3 Toss pasta in large bowl with sauce.

prep & cook time 25 minutes **serves** 4
nutritional count per serving 37.1g total fat (22.6g saturated fat); 634 cal; 56.3g carbohydrate; 15g protein; 6.7g fiber

fettuccine boscaiola

1lb 2oz fettuccine pasta
2 teaspoons olive oil
7oz button mushrooms, sliced thickly
2 cloves garlic, crushed
7oz shaved ham, chopped coarsely
¼ cup (60ml) dry white wine
1¼ cups (300ml) cream
2 tablespoons coarsely chopped fresh chives

1 Cook pasta in large saucepan of boiling water until tender; drain.
2 Meanwhile, heat oil in large saucepan; cook mushrooms, garlic and ham, stirring, until browned lightly. Add wine; boil, uncovered, until wine reduces by half.
3 Add cream to mushroom mixture; reduce heat. Simmer, uncovered, until sauce thickens slightly.
4 Add chives and pasta to sauce; toss to combine.

prep & cook time 30 minutes **serves** 4
nutritional count per serving 38.1g total fat (22.7g saturated fat); 822 cal; 87.8g carbohydrate; 26.8g protein; 5.7g fiber

fettuccine with creamy tomato & sausage sauce

6 thick Italian sausages (1lb 10oz)
2 cloves garlic, crushed
14oz can crushed tomatoes
¼ cup (60ml) dry white wine
1¼ cups cream
13oz fettuccine pasta
6 green onions, chopped finely
2 tablespoons fresh sage leaves

1 Cook sausages in heated oiled large frying pan until browned all over and cooked through. Remove sausages from pan; chop coarsely. Cover to keep warm. Drain excess oil from pan.
2 Combine garlic, undrained tomatoes, wine and cream in same pan; bring to the boil. Reduce heat; simmer, uncovered, about 10 minutes or until sauce thickens slightly.
3 Meanwhile, cook pasta in large saucepan of boiling water until tender; drain. Divide among serving bowls.
4 Stir sausage, onion and sage into tomato mixture; spoon sauce over pasta.

prep & cook time 40 minutes **serves** 4
nutritional count per serving 74.8g total fat (41.2g saturated fat); 1147 cal; 76.2g carbohydrate; 37.1g protein; 8.2g fiber

For a milder-flavored pesto, substitute baby spinach leaves for the rocket.

fettuccine with rocket pesto & tomato salsa

1lb 2oz fettuccine pasta
8 cloves garlic, quartered
½ cup coarsely chopped fresh basil
4oz rocket leaves, chopped coarsely
⅔ cup (160ml) olive oil
½ cup (1oz) finely grated Parmesan cheese
3 medium tomatoes (1lb), chopped coarsely
2 tablespoons lemon juice
2 fresh small red thai chilies, sliced thinly
⅓ cup (2oz) roasted pine nuts

1 Cook pasta in large saucepan of boiling water until tender; drain.
2 Meanwhile to make rocket pesto, blend or process garlic, basil, rocket and oil until smooth.
3 Combine pasta, rocket pesto, cheese, tomato, juice and chili in large saucepan; stir over medium heat until hot. Add nuts; toss gently to combine.

prep & cook time 25 minutes **serves** 4
nutritional count per serving 50.1g total fat (8g saturated fat); 904 cal; 88.9g carbohydrate; 21.1g protein; 7.3g fiber

fettuccine with summer tomato sauce

13oz fettuccine pasta
2 large tomatoes (1lb 2oz), chopped finely
1 medium white onion (5oz), chopped finely
6 seeded green olives, chopped finely
1 tablespoon rinsed, drained capers, chopped finely
2 teaspoons finely chopped fresh oregano
⅓ cup finely chopped fresh flat-leaf parsley
2 cloves garlic, crushed
¼ cup (60ml) olive oil

1 Cook pasta in large saucepan of boiling water until tender; drain.
2 Meanwhile, place remaining ingredients in large bowl; mix well.
3 Add pasta to tomato mixture; toss gently.

prep & cook time 20 minutes **serves** 4
nutritional count per serving 15.1g total fat (2.2g saturated fat); 489 cal; 72.2g carbohydrate; 12.6g protein; 5.8g fiber

beef & red wine casserole

2 cups (500ml) water
2lbs 4oz skirt steak, trimmed,
    cut into cubes
2 medium onions (11oz), sliced thickly
2 tablespoons olive oil
6 cloves garlic, crushed
2 cups (500ml) beef stock
2 cups (500ml) dry red wine
½ cup (5oz) tomato paste
1 tablespoon finely chopped fresh rosemary
1 tablespoon finely chopped fresh flat-leaf parsley
1lb 2oz fresh fettuccine pasta

1 Combine the water, steak, onion, oil, garlic, stock,
wine and paste in deep 12-cup microwave-safe
dish; cook, covered, on HIGH (100%) for 50 minutes, stirring
every 15 minutes to ensure steak remains covered in liquid.
Uncover; cook on HIGH (100%) about 10 minutes or until
steak is tender. Stir in herbs.
2 During final 10 minutes of casserole cooking time, cook
pasta in large saucepan of boiling water until tender; drain.
3 Top pasta with beef and sauce.

prep & cook time 1 hour 20 minutes **serves** 4
nutritional count per serving 16.3g total fat
(4.1g saturated fat); 720 cal; 51.5g carbohydrate;
67.5g protein; 5.3g fiber

fettuccine with meatballs

1lb 2oz lean ground beef
1 cup (3oz) stale breadcrumbs
2 tablespoons finely chopped fresh flat-leaf parsley
2 tablespoons finely chopped fresh chives
1 egg
1 teaspoon Worcestershire sauce
2 teaspoons olive oil
1lb 2oz fettuccine pasta
rosemary paprika sauce
1lb 13oz canned crushed tomatoes
2 cup (500ml) water
⅓ cup (40ml) dry red wine
2 medium onions (11oz), chopped finely
1 teaspoon Worcestershire sauce
2 teaspoons sweet paprika
6 sprigs fresh rosemary

1 Make rosemary paprika sauce.
2 Combine beef, breadcrumbs, parsley, chives, egg and sauce in large bowl; shape into small meatballs.
3 Heat oil in medium saucepan; cook meatballs, in batches, until browned all over and cooked through. Drain on absorbent paper.
4 Meanwhile, cook pasta in large saucepan of boiling water until tender; drain.
5 Add meatballs to sauce; mix well. Stir until heated through. Serve pasta with meatballs and sauce.
rosemary paprika sauce Combine ingredients in large saucepan; bring to the boil. Reduce heat; simmer, uncovered, about 20 minutes or until thickened slightly.

prep & cook time 1 hour **serves** 4
nutritional count per serving 34.1g total fat (8.4g saturated fat); 953 cal; 108.8g carbohydrate; 44.2g protein; 8.6g fiber

salmon fettuccine in creamy lime sauce

13oz fettuccine pasta
1 tablespoon olive oil
4 x 8oz salmon fillets, skinned
1 small onion (3oz), chopped finely
1 clove garlic, crushed
2 teaspoons finely grated lime rind
1 tablespoon lime juice
¼ cup (60ml) dry white wine
1¼ cups (300ml) cream
½ teaspoon drained pink peppercorns, crushed
⅓ cup coarsely chopped fresh chives

1 Cook pasta in large saucepan of boiling water until tender; drain.
2 Meanwhile, heat half the oil in large frying pan; cook fish until browned both sides and cooked as desired. Place fish in large bowl; flake into large pieces.
3 Heat remaining oil in same pan; cook onion and garlic, stirring, until onion softens. Add rind, juice and wine; bring to the boil. Boil, stirring, until liquid reduces to about 2 tablespoons. Stir in cream and peppercorns; return to the boil. Remove from heat.
4 Combine pasta and chives in large bowl with fish, drizzle with sauce; toss gently.

prep & cook time 45 minutes **serves** 4
nutritional count per serving 53.7g total fat (25.8g saturated fat); 990 cal; 67.5g carbohydrate; 55.3g protein; 3.7g fiber

veal scaloppine with rocket & pistachio pesto

1lb 5oz piece veal rump, sliced thinly
1 tablespoon olive oil
¼ cup (60ml) dry white wine
2 teaspoons finely grated lemon rind
1 clove garlic, crushed
13oz fettuccine pasta
rocket & pistachio pesto
2oz baby rocket leaves, trimmed
½ cup (3oz) pistachios, roasted
⅓ cup (1oz) coarsely grated Parmesan cheese
1 clove garlic, quartered
1 tablespoon lemon juice
¾ cup (180ml) olive oil

1 Combine veal, oil, wine, rind and garlic in medium bowl. Cover; refrigerate 2 hours.
2 Make rocket & pistachio pesto.
3 Cook pasta in large saucepan of boiling water until tender; drain.
4 Meanwhile, cook veal, in batches, under preheated grill until browned all over and cooked as desired.
5 Combine pasta in large bowl with half the pesto; toss gently. Serve veal on pasta topped with remaining pesto.
rocket & pistachio pesto Blend or process rocket, nuts, cheese and garlic until well combined. With motor operating, gradually add combined juice and oil in a thin steady stream; blend until pesto thickens slightly.

prep & cook time 25 minutes (+ refrigeration) **serves** 4
nutritional count per serving 58.9g total fat (9.4g saturated fat); 1014 cal; 67g carbohydrate; 49.9g protein; 5g fiber

fettuccine with mushrooms and chili

2 tablespoons olive oil
1lb 2oz button mushrooms, sliced thinly
2 fresh long red chilies, sliced thinly
1 clove garlic, crushed
1lb 2oz fettuccine pasta
⅓ cup (80ml) olive oil, extra
4oz baby spinach leaves

1 Heat oil in large frying pan; cook mushrooms, stirring, 10 minutes or until tender. Add chili and garlic; cook, stirring, until fragrant.
2 Meanwhile, cook pasta in large saucepan of boiling water until tender. Drain, reserving ⅓ cup of the cooking liquid.
3 Place mushroom mixture and pasta in large bowl with extra oil, spinach and reserved cooking liquid; toss gently.

prep & cook time 25 minutes **serves** 4
nutritional count per serving 29.2g total fat (4.1g saturated fat); 700 cal; 85.9g carbohydrate; 19.2g protein; 8.1g fiber

fettuccine with cauliflower and broccoli

4oz butter
4 cloves garlic, crushed
½ cup (1oz) stale breadcrumbs
2 drained anchovy fillets, chopped coarsely
4 cups (13oz) coarsely chopped cauliflower
4 cups (13oz) coarsely chopped broccoli
9oz fettuccine pasta

1 Heat butter in large frying pan; cook garlic and breadcrumbs, stirring, until breadcrumbs are browned. Stir in anchovy.
2 Meanwhile, bring large saucepan of water to the boil. Add cauliflower and broccoli; cook, stirring, to ensure pieces separate. When vegetables are just tender, drain; rinse under cold water, drain.
3 Cook pasta in large saucepan of boiling water until tender; drain.
4 Place pasta in large bowl with cauliflower, broccoli and breadcrumb mixture; toss gently.

prep & cook time 30 minutes **serves** 4
nutritional count per serving 27.2g total fat (17.1g saturated fat); 526 cal; 51.3g carbohydrate; 15.1g protein; 8.1g fiber

chicken pizzaiola with fettuccine

⅓ cup (80ml) olive oil

2 cloves garlic, crushed

½ cup (125ml) dry white wine

½ cup (125ml) chicken stock

2 x 14oz cans crushed tomatoes

2 tablespoons coarsely chopped fresh oregano

2 tablespoons coarsely chopped fresh flat-leaf parsley

½ cup (3oz) pitted kalamata olives

4 chicken thigh fillets (1lb 13oz)

¼ cup (1oz) all-purpose flour

2 eggs

1 tablespoon milk

1 cup (3oz) stale breadcrumbs

7 slices prosciutto (4oz)

1¾ cups (6oz) grated mozzarella cheese

9oz fettuccine pasta

1 Preheat oven to 400°F.

2 Heat half the oil in medium frying pan; cook garlic, stirring, over low heat, until fragrant. Add wine and stock; bring to the boil. Reduce heat; simmer, uncovered, 3 minutes. Add undrained tomatoes, oregano and parsley; bring to the boil. Reduce heat; simmer, uncovered, about 10 minutes or until pizzaiola sauce thickens slightly. Stir in olives.

3 Meanwhile, toss chicken in flour; shake away excess. Dip chicken, one at a time, in combined eggs and milk, then breadcrumbs. Heat remaining oil in large frying pan; cook chicken, in batches, until browned lightly.

4 Place chicken, in single layer, in medium shallow baking dish; top with prosciutto, sauce, then the cheese. Bake, uncovered, in oven about 20 minutes or until chicken is cooked through.

5 Meanwhile, cook pasta in large saucepan of boiling water until tender; drain. Serve pasta topped with chicken pizzaiola.

prep & cook time 1 hour **serves** 4
nutritional count per serving 46.2g total fat (14.2g saturated fat); 1014 cal; 72.5g carbohydrate; 69.4g protein; 6.1g fiber

fettuccine with green olives and lemon

1lb 2oz fettuccine pasta
1oz butter
4 cloves garlic, crushed
9oz small pimiento-stuffed green olives
2oz butter, chopped, extra
1 cup (3oz) finely grated Parmesan cheese
⅓ cup coarsely chopped fresh flat-leaf parsley
2 teaspoons grated lemon rind
2 tablespoons lemon juice

1 Cook pasta in large saucepan of boiling water until tender. Drain, reserving ½ cup of the cooking liquid. Return pasta to pan.
2 Meanwhile, heat butter in small frying pan; cook garlic and olives, stirring, until garlic is soft and olives are heated through.
3 Add olive mixture to pasta with extra butter, cheese, parsley, rind and juice; toss gently. Stir in enough of the reserved cooking liquid to moisten.

prep & cook time 20 minutes **serves** 4
nutritional count per serving 29.6g total fat (15.9g saturated fat); 726 cal; 87.2g carbohydrate; 22.6g protein; 9.8g fiber

fettuccine with char-grilled vegetables

1lb 2oz fettuccine pasta
2 x 10oz jars antipasto char-grilled vegetables
7oz baby spinach leaves
1 cup (3oz) flaked Parmesan cheese

1 Cook pasta in large saucepan of boiling water until tender; drain.
2 Meanwhile, drain vegetables; reserve ¼ cup of the oil. Chop vegetables coarsely. Cook vegetables with reserved oil in large saucepan until heated through.
3 Toss hot pasta with vegetable mixture, spinach and half the cheese. Serve topped with remaining cheese.

prep & cook time 20 minutes **serves** 4
nutritional count per serving 12.4g total fat (4.9g saturated fat); 767 cal; 119.1g carbohydrate; 33.5g protein; 19.5g fiber

fettuccine with roasted squash and pancetta

2lbs 4oz butternut squash, chopped finely
2 tablespoons olive oil
2 cloves garlic, sliced thinly
4 baby onions (4oz), quartered
12 small fresh sage leaves
12 slices pancetta (6oz)
13oz fettuccine pasta
1 cup (250ml) cream
3 egg yolks
½ cup (1oz) finely grated Parmesan cheese
½ cup finely chopped fresh chives
⅔ cup (2oz) grated Parmesan cheese, extra

1 Preheat oven to 475°F.
2 Combine squash and oil in large baking dish. Roast squash 10 minutes. Add garlic, onions and sage to dish; bake a further 15 minutes or until squash is tender.
3 Place pancetta on an oven tray; place in oven for the last 5 minutes of squash cooking time or until crisp.
4 Meanwhile, cook pasta in large saucepan of boiling water until tender; drain. Return to pan.
5 Combine cream, egg yolks and cheese in medium bowl. Stir through hot pasta, squash mixture and chives. Divide among serving bowls; top with pancetta and extra cheese.

prep & cook time 45 minutes **serves** 4
nutritional count per serving 53.5g total fat (27.5g saturated fat); 977 cal; 84.4g carbohydrate; 36.4g protein; 6.9g fiber

pork and sage with fettuccine

cooking-oil spray
4oz shaved ham
1 tablespoon fresh sage leaves
8 pork cutlets (14oz)
9oz fettuccine pasta
1 cup (250ml) dry white wine
1 tablespoon brown sugar
5oz baby spinach leaves
1 small red onion (4oz), sliced thinly
2 tablespoons finely chopped fresh chives
1 tablespoon olive oil

1 Spray heated large frying pan with cooking oil, add ham; cook, stirring, until browned. Remove from pan; cover to keep warm. Add sage to same pan; cook until just wilted. Remove from pan.
2 Cook pork in same heated oiled pan until browned and just cooked through. Cover to keep warm.
3 Meanwhile, cook pasta in large saucepan of boiling water until tender; drain.
4 Add wine and sugar to same frying pan, bring to the boil; boil until sauce is reduced by one-third.
5 Place pasta in large bowl with spinach, onion, chives and oil; toss gently. Serve pasta mixture topped with pork, ham and sage; drizzle with wine sauce.

prep & cook time 30 minutes **serves** 4
nutritional count per serving 8.1g total fat (1.6g saturated fat); 457 cal; 47.6g carbohydrate; 35.8g protein; 3.4g fiber

fettuccine boscaiola with chicken

1lb 2oz fettuccine pasta
1 tablespoon olive oil
1 medium onion (4oz), chopped finely
5oz bacon, chopped finely
7oz button mushrooms, sliced thinly
¼ cup (60ml) dry white wine
⅔ cup (160ml) cream
1 cup (250ml) milk
1 cup (6oz) thinly sliced cooked chicken
¼ cup (1oz) finely grated Parmesan cheese
2 tablespoons coarsely chopped fresh flat-leaf parsley

1 Cook pasta in large saucepan of boiling water until just tender; drain, reserving ½ cup of cooking liquid.
2 Meanwhile, heat oil in large saucepan; cook onion, stirring, until soft. Add bacon and mushrooms; cook, stirring, 1 minute.
3 Add wine, cream and milk to pan; bring to the boil. Reduce heat, simmer, stirring, 5 minutes. Add chicken; stir until combined.
4 Add pasta to pan with cheese, parsley and reserved cooking liquid; toss gently over low heat until hot. Serve sprinkled with freshly ground black pepper, if desired.

prep & cook time 20 minutes **serves** 4
nutritional count per serving 31.5g total fat (16.2g saturated fat); 816 cal; 91.7g carbohydrate; 35.6g protein; 6g fiber

fettuccine with ham, spinach and asparagus

13oz fettuccine pasta
1oz butter
9oz leg ham, sliced thinly
7oz asparagus, trimmed, chopped coarsely
1 teaspoon cracked black pepper
1 clove garlic, crushed
1oz butter, chopped, extra
6oz baby spinach leaves
½ cup (1oz) flaked Parmesan cheese
lemon wedges, for serving

1 Cook pasta in large saucepan of boiling water until tender; drain. Reserve ⅓ cup cooking liquid.
2 Heat butter in large frying pan; cook ham, asparagus, pepper and garlic, stirring, until asparagus is just tender.
3 Place pasta and ham mixture in large bowl with extra butter, spinach, half the cheese and the reserved liquid; toss until spinach is just wilted.
4 Serve pasta topped with remaining cheese; accompany with lemon wedges.

prep & cook time 20 minutes **serves** 4
nutritional count per serving 19g total fat (11.2g saturated fat); 555 cal; 64.9g carbohydrate; 28.1g protein; 4.9g fiber

smoked cod with rocket pesto and fettuccine

13oz fettuccine pasta
1lb 2oz smoked cod fillets
rocket pesto
5oz baby rocket leaves
2 cloves garlic, crushed
¼ cup (1oz) roasted pine nuts
¼ cup (1oz) roasted unsalted pistachios
2 tablespoons lemon juice
½ cup (1oz) coarsely grated Parmesan cheese
¾ cup (180ml) olive oil

1 Cook pasta in large saucepan of boiling water until tender; drain.
2 Cook fish in large frying pan until browned both sides; cool 5 minutes then flake with fork into large bowl.
3 Make rocket pesto.
4 Add pasta to fish with pesto; toss gently.
rocket pesto Blend or process ingredients to form a smooth paste.

prep & cook time 30 minutes **serves** 4
nutritional count per serving 58.2g total fat (9.3g saturated fat); 967 cal; 67g carbohydrate; 42g protein; 5.2g fiber

chili squid fettuccine

1lb 2oz fettuccine pasta
½ cup (125ml) olive oil
1lb small squid hoods, sliced thinly
2 fresh long red chilies, sliced thinly
2 cloves garlic, crushed
9oz rocket leaves, torn
4oz feta cheese, crumbled

1 Cook pasta in large saucepan of boiling water until tender; drain.
2 Meanwhile, heat 1 tablespoon of the oil in large frying pan; cook squid, in batches, over high heat, until tender and browned lightly.
3 Add remaining oil to pan; cook chili and garlic, stirring, until fragrant. Add rocket; cook, stirring, until just wilted.
4 Place pasta in large bowl with squid, rocket mixture and cheese; toss gently.

prep & cook time 20 minutes **serves** 4
nutritional count per serving 37.5g total fat (8.5g saturated fat); 853 cal; 86.9g carbohydrate; 39g protein; 5.4g fiber

mixed mushroom stroganoff

13oz fettuccine pasta
1 tablespoon olive oil
1oz butter
3 shallots (3oz), sliced thinly
2 cloves garlic, sliced thinly
3 teaspoons smoked paprika
2 tablespoons Dijon mustard
13oz button mushrooms, sliced thinly
7oz Swiss brown mushrooms, sliced thinly
7oz shiitake mushrooms, sliced thinly
¼ cup (60ml) dry white wine
¾ cup (180ml) vegetable stock
1 cup (9oz) sour cream

1 Cook pasta in large saucepan of boiling water until tender; drain.
2 Meanwhile, heat oil and half the butter in large saucepan, add shallots and garlic; cook, stirring, until shallot softens. Add paprika and mustard; cook, stirring, 1 minute. Stir in mushrooms and remaining butter. Cover; cook 10 minutes, stirring occasionally. Add wine and stock; cook, uncovered, about 5 minutes or until liquid is reduced slightly. Add sour cream; simmer gently, uncovered, 5 minutes. Serve over pasta.

prep & cook time 40 minutes **serves** 4
nutritional count per serving 34.4g total fat (19.3g saturated fat); 685 cal; 68.7g carbohydrate; 18.8g protein; 8.3g fiber

gnocchi

From the Italian word for dumplings, gnocchi are little balls of dough – great for soaking up delicious pasta sauces.

breaded veal cutlets with gnocchi in mushroom sauce

2 eggs, beaten lightly
2 tablespoons milk
¼ cup (1oz) all-purpose flour
¾ cup (3oz) packaged breadcrumbs
¾ cup (2oz) stale breadcrumbs
¾ cup (3oz) pizza cheese
½ cup coarsely chopped fresh flat-leaf parsley
8 veal cutlets (2lbs 4oz)
¼ cup (60ml) olive oil
2 cloves garlic, sliced thinly
9oz Swiss brown mushrooms, sliced thinly
¾ cup (180ml) cream
½ cup (125ml) beef stock
1lb 6oz fresh potato gnocchi

1 Whisk egg, milk and flour in medium bowl. Combine crumbs, cheese and ⅓ cup of the parsley in another bowl. Coat cutlets in egg mixture then cheese mixture. Place cutlets, in single layer, on tray; refrigerate 10 minutes.
2 Heat half the oil in large frying pan; cook cutlets until browned both sides and cooked as desired. Cover.
3 Heat remaining oil in same pan; cook garlic and mushrooms, stirring, until just tender. Add cream and stock; bring to the boil. Reduce heat; simmer, stirring, until sauce thickens slightly.
4 Meanwhile, cook gnocchi in large saucepan of boiling water until they float to the surface and are just tender; drain, place in large bowl. Stir remaining parsley into sauce and pour over gnocchi; toss to combine. Serve gnocchi with cutlets.

prep & cook time 50 minutes **serves** 4
nutritional count per serving 47.1g total fat (20.6g saturated fat); 955 cal; 62.4g carbohydrate; 67g protein; 6.6g fiber

To make this a meal suitable for vegetarians, substitute vegetable stock for the chicken stock. Fresh potato gnocchi is available from the refrigerated section of most supermarkets.

gnocchi with caramelized squash & sage sauce

1lb 2oz butternut squash, cut into ½in cubes
¼ cup (60ml) chicken stock (*see note, above*)
1 large leek (1lb 2oz), sliced thinly
1 tablespoon brown sugar
1½ cups (375ml) water
2 teaspoons finely chopped fresh sage
½ cup (125ml) low-fat evaporated milk
2lb 4oz fresh potato gnocchi

1 Preheat oven to 425°F.
2 Place squash in oiled baking dish; bake, uncovered, about 30 minutes or until squash is tender.
3 Bring stock to the boil in large saucepan, add leek; cook, stirring, until leek softens. Add squash and sugar; cook, stirring, about 10 minutes or until squash caramelizes. Stir in the water, sage and milk; blend or process squash mixture, in batches, until smooth. Return squash sauce to same pan; stir over heat until hot.
4 Meanwhile, cook gnocchi in large saucepan of boiling water until they float to the surface and are just tender; drain. Toss hot gnocchi through hot squash sauce.

prep & cook time 55 minutes **serves** 4
nutritional count per serving 1.7g total fat (0.5g saturated fat); 421 cal; 79.3g carbohydrate; 16.9g protein; 8.2g fiber

You will need to buy a piece of unpeeled pumpkin weighing about 1lb 7oz for this recipe.

gnocchi with roasted pumpkin & burnt butter sauce

1lb 2oz trimmed pumpkin, cut into ½in cubes
2lb 4oz fresh potato gnocchi
4oz butter
1 tablespoon olive oil
1 clove garlic, crushed
1 tablespoon finely shredded fresh sage

1 Preheat oven to 350°F.
2 Place pumpkin on oiled oven tray; roast about
15 minutes or until just tender.
3 Cook gnocchi in large saucepan of boiling water until
they float to the surface and are just tender; drain.
4 Meanwhile, melt butter with oil in medium frying pan;
cook garlic, stirring, 2 minutes. Add sage; cook, stirring,
until butter foams.
5 Combine pumpkin, gnocchi and butter mixture in large
bowl; stir gently.

prep & cook time 20 minutes **serves** 4
nutritional count per serving 27.8g total fat
(15.5g saturated fat); 644 cal; 81g carbohydrate;
13.3g protein; 7.4g fiber

gnocchi with tomato & basil sauce

4 cups milk

1 cup (6oz) semolina

4 egg yolks

⅔ cup (2oz) finely grated Parmesan cheese

2 tablespoons semolina, extra

2 tablespoons olive oil

4 cloves garlic, crushed

½ cup coarsely chopped fresh basil

2 cups bottled tomato sauce

1oz butter, melted

½ cup (1oz) finely grated Parmesan cheese, extra

1 Bring milk to the boil in medium saucepan. Gradually add semolina, stirring constantly. Reduce heat; simmer, stirring, about 5 minutes or until mixture thickens. Remove from heat; stir in egg yolks and cheese. Stand 5 minutes.

2 Sprinkle extra semolina on flat surface; roll mixture into two 5cm-thick sausage shapes. Wrap in plastic; refrigerate 1 hour or until firm.

3 Meanwhile, heat oil in small saucepan; cook garlic and basil, stirring, until fragrant. Add pasta sauce; bring to the boil. Reduce heat; simmer, covered, 2 minutes.

4 Preheat grill. Cut semolina into ¾in gnocchi pieces. Place gnocchi, in single layer, on oiled oven trays. Brush gnocchi with melted butter; sprinkle with extra cheese. Grill about 3 minutes or until cheese browns lightly.

5 Serve gnocchi topped with tomato sauce; sprinkle with fresh basil leaves, if desired.

prep & cook time 30 minutes (+ refrigeration) **serves** 6
nutritional count per serving 27.9g total fat
(13.2g saturated fat); 495 cal; 40.9g carbohydrate;
18.8g protein; 3.3g fiber

ricotta gnocchi in fresh tomato sauce

1lb 2oz firm ricotta cheese
1 cup (3oz) finely grated Parmesan cheese
½ cup (3oz) all-purpose flour
2 eggs, beaten lightly
1 tablespoon olive oil
4 medium tomatoes (1lb 11oz), chopped coarsely
6 green onions, sliced thinly
2 tablespoons coarsely chopped fresh oregano
2 tablespoons balsamic vinegar
2 tablespoons olive oil, extra
½ cup (1oz) shaved Parmesan cheese

1 Combine ricotta, grated Parmesan, flour, egg and oil in large bowl.
2 Drop rounded tablespoons of mixture into boiling water; cook until gnocchi float to the surface and are just tender; drain, cover to keep warm.
3 Combine tomato, onion, oregano and vinegar in medium bowl.
4 Divide warm gnocchi among serving bowls, top with fresh tomato sauce; drizzle with extra oil, sprinkle with shaved Parmesan.

prep & cook time 30 minutes **serves** 4
nutritional count per serving 40.6g total fat (18g saturated fat); 570 cal; 19.4g carbohydrate; 32.1g protein; 3.3g fiber

gnocchi with herb and mushroom sauce

1 tablespoon vegetable oil
1 medium onion (5oz), chopped coarsely
2 cloves garlic, crushed
14oz Swiss brown mushrooms, sliced thinly
1 tablespoon all-purpose flour
⅓ cup (80ml) dry red wine
2 teaspoons soy sauce
⅔ cup (160ml) vegetable stock
1 tablespoon sour cream
1 tablespoon coarsely chopped fresh oregano
1 tablespoon finely chopped fresh sage
1lb 5oz fresh potato gnocchi

1 Heat oil in large frying pan; cook onion, garlic and mushrooms, stirring, until vegetables are just tender. Add flour; cook, stirring, 1 minute.
2 Add wine, sauce, stock and cream to pan; cook, stirring, until sauce thickens slightly. Stir in herbs.
3 Meanwhile, cook gnocchi in large saucepan of boiling water until gnocchi rise to the surface and are just tender; drain. Add gnocchi to herb and mushroom sauce; toss gently to combine.

prep & cook time 25 minutes **serves** 4
nutritional count per serving 8.5g total fat (2.6g saturated fat); 347 cal; 48.6g carbohydrate; 11.6g protein; 6.8g fiber

baked sweet potato gnocchi with garlic cream sauce

2 large sweet potatoes (2lb 4oz), chopped coarsely
4 small white potatoes (1lb 1oz), chopped coarsely
1½ cups (8oz) plain flour
1 teaspoon ground nutmeg
½ cup (3oz) roasted pine nuts
1 cup (3oz) finely grated Parmesan cheese
garlic cream sauce
2½ cups (600ml) cream
2 cloves garlic, crushed

1 Preheat oven to 350°F.
2 Roast sweet potato and white potato, in single layer, on oiled oven tray about 1 hour or until vegetables are tender; cool.
3 Make garlic cream sauce.
4 Increase oven temperature to 400°F.
Lightly oil six 2-cup (500ml) ovenproof dishes.
5 Mash sweet potato and white potato in large bowl until smooth; add sifted flour and nutmeg, stir to a soft, sticky dough.

6 Divide dough into quarters; flatten each quarter on floured surface to ½in thickness. Cut 2in rounds from dough; transfer gnocchi to tea towel-lined tray. Reshape and cut rounds from any remaining dough until all dough is used.
7 Cook gnocchi, in four batches, in large saucepan of boiling water until gnocchi rise to the surface and are just tender; drain.
8 Divide gnocchi among dishes, top with sauce, pine nuts and cheese. Cook, in oven, about 15 minutes or until golden brown. If you like, top with a little extra finely grated Parmesan cheese to serve.
garlic cream sauce Combine cream and garlic in medium frying pan; bring to the boil. Reduce heat; simmer, uncovered, about 5 minutes or until thickened slightly.

prep & cook time 1 hour 45 minutes (+ cooling)
serves 6
nutritional count per serving 57.6g total fat (32g saturated fat); 831 cal; 59.4g carbohydrate; 17.2g protein; 5.9g fiber

You can make the gnocchi and leave it, covered, at room temperature for several hours ahead of cooking.

creamy pesto chicken with gnocchi

2lb chicken thigh fillets
1 tablespoon olive oil
2 cloves garlic, crushed
2 shallots (2oz), chopped finely
4oz fresh shiitake mushrooms, sliced thickly
½ cup (125ml) dry white wine
¼ cup (3oz) sun-dried tomato pesto
1¼ cups (300ml) light cream
⅓ cup coarsely chopped fresh basil
1lb 6oz fresh potato gnocchi

1 Cut each chicken fillet into thirds. Heat oil in large frying pan; cook chicken, in batches, until cooked through. Cover to keep warm.
2 Add garlic, shallot and mushrooms to same pan; cook, stirring, 2 minutes. Stir in wine; simmer, uncovered, until liquid is almost evaporated. Stir in pesto and cream; bring to the boil. Remove from heat; stir in basil.
3 Meanwhile, cook gnocchi in large saucepan of boiling water until they rise to the surface and are just tender; drain.
4 Divide gnocchi and chicken among serving plates; drizzle with creamy pesto.

prep & cook time 35 minutes **serves** 4
nutritional counter serving 49.2g total fat (20.9g saturated fat); 880 cal; 52.1g carbohydrate; 52.9g protein; 5g fiber

gnocchi al quattro formaggi

¼ cup (60ml) dry white wine
1 cup (9oz) mascarpone cheese
1 cup (4oz) coarsely grated mozzarella cheese
½ cup (1oz) coarsely grated Parmesan cheese
¼ cup (60ml) milk
1lb 6oz fresh potato gnocchi
3oz gorgonzola cheese, crumbled

1 Add wine to large saucepan; bring to the boil. Boil, uncovered, until wine reduces by half. Reduce heat, add mascarpone; stir until mixture is smooth. Add mozzarella, Parmesan and milk; cook, stirring, until cheeses melt and sauce is smooth.
2 Meanwhile, cook gnocchi in large saucepan of boiling water until they rise to the surface and are just tender; drain.
3 Add gnocchi and gorgonzola to sauce; toss gently.

prep & cook time 20 minutes **serves** 4
nutritional count per serving 59.5g total fat (39.1g saturated fat); 786 cal; 28.8g carbohydrate; 32g protein; 2.2g fiber

Serve this pasta dish with grilled chops or poached fish fillets for a delicious main meal.

lasagna & cannelloni

This classic Italian dish of layers of pasta, meat and cheese sauce is the ideal recipe to make when you're entertaining as most of the work can be done well in advance.

four cheese lasagna

2 teaspoons olive oil
1 medium onion (5oz), chopped finely
2 cloves garlic, crushed
1lb 2oz lean ground beef
2 x 15oz cans crushed tomatoes
½ cup (5oz) tomato paste
½ teaspoon white sugar
½ cup finely chopped fresh basil
¼ cup finely chopped fresh oregano
1lb 2oz ricotta cheese
1 cup (3oz) finely grated Parmesan cheese
1 cup (4oz) coarsely grated mozzarella cheese
¼ teaspoon ground nutmeg
4 eggs
7oz large instant lasagna sheets
1 cup (4oz) pizza cheese

1 Heat oil in large saucepan; cook onion and garlic, stirring, until onion softens. Add mince; cook, stirring, until mince changes color. Add undrained tomatoes, paste and sugar; cook, stirring, until sauce thickens. Remove from heat; stir in basil and oregano.
2 Preheat oven to 350°F.
3 Beat ricotta, Parmesan, mozzarella and nutmeg in medium bowl with electric mixer until well combined. Add eggs, one at a time, beating until just combined between additions.
4 Place a third of the lasagna sheets in shallow 10-cup baking dish; top with half the meat sauce and half the cheese mixture. Top with another third of the lasagna sheets, remaining meat sauce, remaining lasagna sheets then remaining cheese mixture. Top with pizza cheese.
5 Bake, uncovered, about 45 minutes or until cheese browns lightly. Stand lasagna 5 minutes before serving.

prep & cook time 1 hour 20 minutes **serves** 6
nutritional count per serving 32.7g total fat (17.2g saturated fat); 639 cal; 33.2g carbohydrate; 50.9g protein; 4.1g fiber

lasagna with pesto

1oz butter
¼ cup (1oz) pine nuts
1 cup firmly packed fresh basil leaves
1 clove garlic, crushed
2 tablespoons grated Parmesan cheese
1 teaspoon white sugar
½ cup (125ml) olive oil
13oz fresh lasagna sheets, sliced thickly

1 Melt butter in small saucepan. Cook nuts, stirring over medium heat, until browned lightly; cool.
2 Process basil, nuts, garlic, cheese and sugar until smooth. While motor is operating, gradually add oil in a thin steady stream; process until combined.
3 Cook pasta in large saucepan of boiling water until tender; drain.
4 Stir pesto through pasta to serve.

prep & cook time 25 minutes **serves** 4
nutritional count per serving 39.6g total fat (6.6g saturated fat); 681 cal; 67.6g carbohydrate; 12g protein; 4g fiber

Pesto can be made a week ahead; refrigerate, covered, or freeze for up to three months.

wonton lasagna stacks

1lb 5oz ground beef
2 tablespoons tomato paste
2 green onions, chopped finely
2 eggs
9oz ricotta cheese
2 tablespoons finely shredded fresh basil
12 wonton wrappers
½ cup (2oz) pizza cheese
25oz bottled pasta sauce

1 Preheat oven to 350°F.
2 Combine mince, paste, onion and one egg in medium bowl; shape mixture into eight patties.
3 Combine ricotta, basil and remaining egg in another medium bowl.
4 Place four wrappers, in single layer, in shallow baking dish; top each with a patty. Divide half the ricotta mixture among patties; sprinkle with half the pizza cheese, top with a wrapper; repeat layering ending with a wrapper.
5 Pour sauce over stacks; cook about 50 minutes or until stacks are cooked through and set. Serve with crusty Italian bread and a green salad, if desired.

prep & cook time 1 hour 20 minutes **serves** 4
nutritional count per serving 27.8g total fat (13.3g saturated fat); 521 cal; 19.3g carbohydrate; 46.8g protein; 3.8g fiber

lasagna with tomato sauce

13oz fresh lasagna sheets, sliced thickly
2 tablespoons extra virgin olive oil
6 medium tomatoes (2lb), peeled, seeded,
    chopped coarsely
¼ cup coarsely chopped fresh basil
2 cloves garlic, crushed
2 teaspoons red wine vinegar
1 fresh small red thai chili, chopped finely
3oz low-fat feta cheese, crumbled

1 Cook pasta in large saucepan of boiling water until tender; drain. Sprinkle half the oil over pasta; toss gently.
2 Combine tomato, basil, garlic, remaining oil, vinegar and chili in medium bowl.
3 Divide pasta among serving plates. Spoon tomato mixture over pasta; sprinkle with cheese.

prep & cook time 20 minutes **serves** 8
nutritional count per serving 6.7g total fat
(1.7g saturated fat); 240 cal; 34.2g carbohydrate;
9g protein; 3.1g fiber

To peel tomatoes, slice a cross in the bottom of each tomato, then place in a large bowl of boiling water for 1 minute; drain. Rinse under cold water; peel.

smoked salmon lasagna

8 sheets curly lasagna
14oz thinly sliced smoked salmon
1 medium avocado (9oz), sliced thinly
⅓ cup (80ml) lime juice
½ cup (125ml) peanut oil
1 tablespoon finely chopped fresh dill
2 teaspoons wholegrain mustard
4oz baby spinach leaves

1 Cook pasta in large saucepan of boiling water until tender; drain. Rinse under cold water; drain, then pat dry with absorbent paper.
2 Place two pasta sheets on board; layer half the salmon evenly over sheets. Top salmon with pasta sheets then avocado, pasta sheets, remaining salmon and remaining pasta sheets. Cut stacks in half, then cut in half diagonally. Place two pieces on each serving plate.
3 Place juice, oil, dill and mustard in screw-top jar; shake well. Pour half the dressing over spinach in medium bowl; toss gently. Drizzle stacks with remaining dressing; serve with spinach.

prep & cook time 25 minutes **serves** 4
nutritional count per serving 43.5g total fat
(8.3g saturated fat); 618 cal; 27.4g carbohydrate;
28.9g protein; 2.7g fiber

roasted vegetable lasagna

2 medium eggplants (1lb 5oz), sliced thinly
3 medium red peppers (1lb 5oz)
2 tablespoons coarse cooking salt
2 medium zucchini (9oz), sliced thinly
1lb 5oz sweet potato, sliced thinly
cooking-oil spray
25oz bottled tomato sauce
4 fresh lasagna sheets, trimmed to fit baking dish
5oz firm ricotta, crumbled
1 tablespoon finely grated Parmesan cheese
white sauce
1oz low-fat dairy-free spread
¼ cup (1oz) all-purpose flour
1½ cups (375ml) skim milk
2 tablespoons coarsely grated Parmesan cheese

1 Preheat oven to 475°F.
2 Place eggplant in colander, sprinkle with salt; stand 20 minutes. Rinse eggplant under cold water; pat dry with absorbent paper towel.
3 Meanwhile, quarter peppers; discard seeds and membranes. Roast peppers, uncovered, in hot oven, skin-side up, about 5 minutes or until skin blisters and blackens. Cover pepper pieces in plastic or paper for 5 minutes; peel away skin.
4 Reduce oven temperature to 400°F.

5 Place eggplant, zucchini and sweet potato, in single layer, on oven trays; spray with oil. Roast, uncovered, about 15 minutes or until tender.
6 Meanwhile, make white sauce.
7 Oil deep rectangular 10-cup ovenproof dish. Spread 1 cup pasta sauce over base of prepared dish; top with half the eggplant and half the pepper. Layer with lasagna sheet; top with ½ cup of the pasta sauce, ricotta, sweet potato and zucchini. Layer with another lasagna sheet; top with remaining pasta sauce, remaining eggplant and remaining pepper. Layer remaining lasagna sheet over vegetables; top with white sauce, sprinkle with Parmesan. Bake, uncovered, about 45 minutes or until browned lightly. Stand 5 minutes before serving.
white sauce Melt spread in small saucepan, add flour; cook, stirring, until mixture thickens and bubbles. Remove from heat, gradually stir in milk; cook, stirring, until sauce boils and thickens. Remove from heat; stir in cheese.

prep & cook time 1 hour 40 minutes **serves** 6
nutritional count per serving 9g fat
(3.2g saturated fat); 311 cal; 44.1g carbohydrate; 14.2g protein; 8.1g fiber

Use scissors to trim lasagna sheets to fit into your baking dish; you may only need three sheets in total.

pork and veal lasagna

1 tablespoon olive oil

1 medium onion (5oz), chopped coarsely

3 stalks celery (1lb), trimmed, chopped coarsely

4 cloves garlic, crushed

2 teaspoons ground cinnamon

1lb 13oz ground pork and veal

1 tablespoon all-purpose flour

2 tablespoons red wine vinegar

2 teaspoons brown sugar

3 cups (700ml) bottled tomato sauce

14oz can diced tomatoes

¼ cup finely chopped fresh sage

1oz butter

2 tablespoons all-purpose flour, extra

2½ cups (625ml) hot milk

1½ cups (4oz) finely grated Parmesan cheese

9oz fresh lasagna sheets, trimmed to fit baking dish

2½ cups (9oz) coarsely grated mozzarella cheese

12 fresh sage leaves

1 Heat oil in large saucepan; cook onion and celery, stirring, until soft. Add garlic and cinnamon; cook, stirring, until fragrant.

2 Add mince; cook, stirring, until meat changes color. Add flour; cook, stirring, 1 minute. Stir in vinegar, sugar, pasta sauce and undrained tomatoes; bring to the boil. Reduce heat; simmer, stirring occasionally, about 15 minutes or until sauce thickens. Stir in chopped sage.

3 Preheat oven to 350°F.

4 Meanwhile, melt butter in medium saucepan. Add extra flour; cook, stirring, until mixture thickens and bubbles. Gradually stir in milk; stir until mixture boils and thickens. Remove sauce from heat; stir in one-third of the Parmesan.

5 Spread a quarter of the meat sauce into a shallow 8in x 12in ovenproof dish. Cover with one layer of the trimmed lasagna sheets, then one-third of the remaining meat sauce, half the cheese sauce and half the mozzarella. Make two more layers with the remaining trimmed lasagna sheets and meat sauce; top with remaining cheese sauce then sprinkle with combined remaining cheeses. Sprinkle with sage leaves. Cook lasagna, uncovered, in oven, about 50 minutes or until browned lightly. Stand 15 minutes. Serve with mesclun salad, if you like.

prep & cook time 1 hour 30 minutes (+ standing) **serves** 6

nutritional count per serving 39.3g total fat (20.5g saturated fat); 820 cal; 55.2g carbohydrate; 58.3g protein; 6.3g fiber

Ground pork and veal are often sold as a combination by many butchers. If you buy it as individual packages, you need 14oz of each.
Make both sauces a day ahead then assemble the lasagna when you're ready, or finish the lasagna a day ahead, put it in the fridge, then reheat it in the oven (350°F), covered, for about 30 minutes.
The lasagna can also be frozen whole or in serving-sized portions. The whole lasagna will take about 24 hours to thaw in the refrigerator. Individual portions can be thawed in a microwave oven – follow the manufacturer's directions.

You need to buy a large barbecued chicken weighing approximately 2lb for this recipe.

chicken & leek lasagna

2oz butter
1 large leek (1lb 2oz), sliced thinly
¼ cup (1oz) all-purpose flour
2 teaspoons Dijon mustard
2 cups (500ml) chicken stock, warmed
3 cups (1lb 1oz) shredded barbecued chicken
4 fresh lasagna sheets (7oz), trimmed to fit baking dish
⅔ cup (3oz) coarsely grated cheddar cheese

1 Preheat oven to 350°F.
2 Melt butter in medium saucepan; cook leek, stirring, until soft. Add flour; cook, stirring, until mixture thickens and bubbles. Gradually stir in mustard and stock; stir over medium heat until mixture boils and thickens. Reserve ⅔ cup of the sauce, then stir chicken into remaining sauce.
3 Oil shallow 8-cup baking dish. Cover base with one lasagna sheet; top with about a quarter of the warm chicken mixture. Repeat layering with remaining lasagna and chicken mixture, finishing with chicken mixture; top with reserved sauce and the cheese.
4 Bake, covered, in oven, 30 minutes; uncover, bake about 20 minutes or until browned lightly. Stand 5 minutes before serving.

prep & cook time 1 hour 35 minutes **serves** 4
nutritional count per serving 24.8g total fat (8.5g saturated fat); 403 cal; 15.5g carbohydrate; 28.8g protein; 2.4g fiber

tuna spinach lasagna

1oz butter
2 tablespoons all-purpose flour
1 cup (250ml) milk
¾ cup (3oz) coarsely grated cheddar cheese
4 fresh lasagna sheets (7oz), trimmed to fit baking dish
1 cup (3oz) stale breadcrumbs
tuna spinach mornay
2oz butter
1 medium onion (5oz), sliced thinly
¼ cup (1oz) all-purpose flour
2 cups (500ml) milk, warmed
5oz baby spinach leaves
15oz can tuna in springwater, drained
2 tablespoons lemon juice

1 Preheat oven to 350°F. Oil shallow 8-cup baking dish. Make tuna spinach mornay.
2 Melt butter in small saucepan. Add flour; cook, stirring, until mixture thickens. Gradually stir in milk over medium heat until mixture boils. Stir in a quarter of the cheese.
3 Line dish with one lasagna sheet; top with a third of the mornay. Repeat layering with lasagna and mornay, finishing with lasagna. Spread cheese sauce over top; sprinkle with breadcrumbs and remaining cheese.
4 Bake, covered, 30 minutes; uncover, bake about 20 minutes or until browned lightly. Stand 5 minutes.
tuna spinach mornay Melt butter in pan; cook onion until soft. Add flour; cook, stirring, until mixture thickens. Gradually add milk; stir until mixture boils and thickens. Remove from heat; stir in spinach, tuna and juice.

prep & cook time 1 hour 35 minutes **serves** 4
nutritional count per serving 21.7g total fat (13.4g saturated fat); 428 cal; 30.9g carbohydrate; 26.2g protein; 2.5g fiber

classic lasagna

1 tablespoon olive oil

1 medium onion (5oz), chopped finely

1 medium carrot (4oz), chopped finely

1 stalk celery (5oz), trimmed, chopped finely

2 cloves garlic, crushed

1lb 2oz ground beef

⅓ cup (80ml) dry red wine

1lb 14oz can crushed tomatoes

2 tablespoons tomato paste

½ cup (125ml) water

4 slices prosciutto (2oz), chopped finely

1 tablespoon coarsely chopped fresh oregano

2 tablespoons coarsely chopped fresh flat-leaf parsley

18 instant lasagna sheets

½ cup (1oz) grated Parmesan cheese

cheese sauce

2oz butter

⅓ cup (2oz) all-purpose flour

4 cups milk

¾ cup (2oz) grated Parmesan cheese

pinch ground nutmeg

1 Heat oil in large frying pan; cook onion, carrot, celery and garlic, stirring, until onion is soft. Add beef; cook, stirring, until browned. Add wine; bring to the boil. Stir in undrained tomatoes, paste and the water; reduce heat. Simmer, uncovered, about 1 hour or until mixture is thick. Stir in prosciutto and herbs; cool slightly.

2 Meanwhile, make cheese sauce.

3 Preheat oven to 350°F. Oil shallow 12-cup ovenproof dish.

4 Trim six lasagna sheets to fit prepared dish; place in dish. Spread with half the meat sauce; drizzle with 1 cup of the cheese sauce. Repeat layering; top with remaining pasta sheets then spread with remaining cheese sauce and sprinkle with cheese.

5 Bake about 45 minutes or until pasta is tender and cheese is browned lightly.

cheese sauce Melt butter in heated large saucepan, add flour; cook, stirring, until mixture bubbles and thickens. Remove from heat; gradually stir in milk. Cook, stirring, until mixture boils and thickens. Remove from heat; stir in cheese and nutmeg. Cool 10 minutes.

prep & cook time 2 hours 50 minutes **serves** 6
nutritional count per serving 32.5g total fat (17.2g saturated fat); 716 cal; 62g carbohydrate; 38.7g protein; 5.6g fiber

Recipe can be made up to three days ahead; store, covered, in the refrigerator. Recipe can also be frozen for up to three months.

chicken & prosciutto cannelloni

2oz butter
¼ cup (1oz) all-purpose flour
⅔ cup (160ml) milk
1½ cups (375ml) chicken stock
½ cup (1oz) grated Parmesan cheese
14oz grated mozzarella cheese
1 tablespoon olive oil
2 medium onions (11oz), chopped finely
3 cloves garlic, crushed
2lb 4oz ground chicken
2 tablespoons finely chopped fresh sage
1lb 14oz can crushed tomatoes
½ cup (125ml) dry white wine
¼ cup (3oz) tomato paste
3 teaspoons white sugar
12 fresh lasagna sheets
24 slices prosciutto (13oz), cut in half crossways

1 Melt butter in medium saucepan, add flour; cook, stirring, until mixture thickens and bubbles. Gradually stir in milk and stock; cook, stirring, until sauce boils and thickens. Remove from heat; stir in Parmesan and a quarter of the mozzarella.
2 Heat oil in large saucepan; cook onion and garlic, stirring, until onion is soft. Add chicken; cook, stirring, until browned. Stir in sage. Combine chicken and cheese sauce in large bowl; cool.

3 Combine undrained crushed tomatoes, wine, paste and sugar in same large pan; cook, stirring, 10 minutes. Cool 10 minutes; blend or process, in batches, until smooth.
4 Preheat oven to 350°F.
5 Cut pasta sheets in half crossways. Place two pieces of prosciutto on each piece of pasta. Top each with ¼ cup chicken mixture; roll to enclose filling. Repeat with remaining pasta, prosciutto and chicken mixture.
6 Oil two 12-cup ovenproof dishes. Pour a quarter of the tomato sauce into base of each dish; place half the pasta rolls, seam-side down, in each dish. Pour remaining tomato sauce over rolls; sprinkle with remaining mozzarella.
7 Bake cannelloni, covered, 30 minutes. Uncover, bake a further 15 minutes or until cheese melts and browns. Serve with a green salad, if you like.

prep & cook time 1 hour 40 minutes **serves** 8
nutritional count per serving 36g total fat (18.5g saturated fat); 657 cal; 25.3g carbohydrate; 54.1g protein; 3.2g fiber

Pancetta or double-smoked ham can be substituted for the prosciutto.

eggplant, tomato & leek lasagna

3 medium eggplants (2lb)
coarse cooking salt
1 large onion (7oz), chopped finely
4 cloves garlic, crushed
3 large tomatoes (1lb 8oz), chopped coarsely
2 tablespoons tomato paste
¼ cup finely shredded fresh basil leaves
1 tablespoon butter
2 medium leeks (1lb 9oz), chopped finely
2 tablespoons white sugar
4 fresh lasagna sheets (7oz), trimmed to
     fit 8in-square ovenproof dish
1 cup (4oz) grated cheddar cheese

1 Cut eggplants lengthways into ½in slices; place in colander, sprinkle with salt, stand 30 minutes. Rinse; drain, pat dry. Cook in heated oiled large saucepan until browned.
2 Cook onion and half the garlic in same pan, stirring, until onion softens. Stir in tomato, paste and basil; simmer, uncovered, about 20 minutes or until thickened slightly. Blend or process tomato mixture until just combined.
3 Melt butter in same pan, add leek and remaining garlic; cook, stirring, until leek is soft. Add sugar; cook, stirring, about 5 minutes or until leek is browned lightly.
4 Preheat oven to 400°F. Oil deep 10-cup ovenproof dish.
5 Position one pasta sheet in base of dish; top with a quarter of the eggplant, a quarter of the leek mixture, a quarter of the tomato mixture and a quarter of the cheese. Repeat layers three times, ending with cheese. Bake, uncovered, 50 minutes.

prep & cook time 2 hours 10 minutes (+ standing) **serves** 6
nutritional count per serving 10.7g total fat
(6.1g saturated fat); 333 cal; 40.6g carbohydrate;
13.8g protein; 9.1g fiber

ricotta & swiss chard lasagna

2lb 4oz Swiss chard, trimmed
3 eggs, beaten lightly
2 cups (1lb 1oz) firm ricotta cheese (*see note, below*)
¼ cup (1oz) coarsely grated Parmesan cheese
3 green onions, chopped finely
1½ cups (390ml) bottled tomato sauce
12 sheets instant lasagna sheets
1 cup (4oz) coarsely grated cheddar cheese

1 Preheat oven to 350°F. Oil shallow 12-cup ovenproof dish.
2 Boil, steam or microwave Swiss chard until just wilted; drain. Squeeze as much liquid as possible from Swiss chard; chop coarsely. Combine egg, ricotta, Parmesan and onion in large bowl; stir in Swiss chard.
3 Spread half the pasta sauce over base of ovenproof dish. Cover with three lasagna sheets; top with a third of the Swiss chard mixture. Cover Swiss chard layer with three lasagna sheets; repeat layering with remaining Swiss chard mixture and remaining lasagna sheets. Top lasagna with remaining sauce; sprinkle with cheddar.
4 Cover lasagna with foil; bake 40 minutes. Remove foil; bake a further 20 minutes or until top is browned.

prep & cook time 1 hour 45 minutes **serves** 4
nutritional count per serving 30.9g total fat (17.6g saturated fat); 656 cal; 53.6g carbohydrate; 37.1g protein; 7.6g fiber

You need to use firm ricotta, available from delicatessens, not the soft ricotta in tubs from the refrigerated section of supermarkets.

italian sausage and three cheese lasagna

1lb 2oz Italian sausages

9oz frozen chopped spinach, thawed, drained

9oz ricotta cheese

¼ teaspoon ground nutmeg

½ cup (1oz) finely grated Parmesan cheese

1 egg

6 sheets fresh lasagna sheets, trimmed to fit dish

9 oz mozzarella cheese, sliced thinly

tomato sauce

1 tablespoon olive oil

1 medium onion (5oz), chopped finely

1 medium carrot (4oz), chopped finely

1 stalk celery (5oz), trimmed, chopped finely

5 x 3in long parsley stalks, crushed

2 cloves garlic, crushed

½ cup (125ml) dry red wine

¼ cup (3oz) tomato paste

25oz bottled tomato sauce

cheese sauce

2oz butter

⅓ cup (2oz) all-purpose flour

2 cups (500ml) milk

1½ cups (4oz) finely grated Parmesan cheese

1 Make tomato sauce. Make cheese sauce.

2 Preheat oven to 400°F.

3 Cook sausages in heated oiled large frying pan until browned all over; drain then slice thinly.

4 Combine spinach, ricotta, nutmeg, Parmesan and egg in medium bowl.

5 Spread ½ cup of the cheese sauce over the base of 8in x 12in ovenproof dish. Top with two pasta sheets then spread with half the spinach mixture. Sprinkle with half the sausage; cover with 1 cup of the tomato sauce then half the remaining cheese sauce.

6 Top with two pasta sheets. Spread remaining spinach mixture over pasta; sprinkle with remaining sausage. Spread with 1 cup tomato sauce, then remaining cheese sauce.

7 Top with remaining pasta, then half the remaining tomato sauce. Top with mozzarella; spread with remaining tomato sauce.

8 Bake lasagna, covered, 30 minutes. Uncover, bake about 10 minutes or until browned lightly. Stand 10 minutes before serving.

tomato sauce Heat oil in large saucepan, add onion, carrot, celery and parsley; cook, stirring occasionally, until vegetables soften. Add garlic; cook, stirring, 1 minute. Add wine; cook, stirring, until almost evaporated. Discard parsley stalks. Add paste; cook, stirring, 3 minutes. Add sauce; simmer, uncovered, about 15 minutes.

cheese sauce Melt butter in medium saucepan, add flour; cook, stirring, until mixture thickens and bubbles. Gradually add milk; stir until mixture boils and thickens. Reduce heat; cook, stirring, 1 minute, remove from heat. Add cheese, stir until melted.

prep & cook time 2 hours 40 minutes **serves** 8
nutritional count per serving 46.8g total fat (23.1g saturated fat); 772 cal; 44g carbohydrate; 39.3g protein; 5.4g fiber

spinach and herb cannelloni

2lb 4oz spinach, trimmed, chopped coarsely

1lb 2oz ricotta cheese

2 eggs

1½ cups (4oz) coarsely grated Parmesan cheese

¼ cup finely chopped fresh mint

3 teaspoons finely chopped fresh thyme

2 teaspoons finely chopped fresh rosemary

9oz cannelloni tubes

creamy tomato sauce

1 tablespoon olive oil

1 medium onion (5oz), chopped finely

4 cloves garlic, crushed

4 x 14oz cans diced tomatoes

½ cup (125ml) cream

1 teaspoon white sugar

1 Make creamy tomato sauce.

2 Meanwhile, preheat oven to 350°F.

3 Cook washed, drained (not dried) spinach in heated large saucepan, stirring, until wilted. Drain; when cool enough to handle, squeeze out excess moisture.

4 Combine spinach in large bowl with ricotta, eggs, ½ cup of the Parmesan and the herbs. Using a large piping bag, fill pasta with spinach mixture.

5 Spread a third of the sauce into shallow 10in x 14in ovenproof dish; top with pasta, in single layer, then top with remaining sauce. Cook, covered, in oven, 20 minutes. Uncover, sprinkle pasta with remaining Parmesan; cook about 15 minutes or until pasta is tender and cheese is browned lightly. Serve with a tossed green salad, if you like.

creamy tomato sauce Heat oil in large saucepan; cook onion, stirring, until softened. Add garlic; cook, stirring, until fragrant. Add undrained tomatoes; bring to the boil. Reduce heat; simmer, uncovered, stirring occasionally, about 20 minutes or until sauce thickens slightly. Cool 10 minutes; blend or process sauce with cream and sugar until smooth.

prep & cook time 1 hour **serves** 6
nutritional count per serving 31g total fat (17.1g saturated fat); 577 cal; 41.8g carbohydrate; 28.7g protein; 8.3g fiber

The cannelloni can be prepared completely up to a day ahead, ready to go into the oven. Keep it covered in the refrigerator overnight.

linguine

Linguine ('little tongues') are flat strands of pasta related to fettuccine, but thinner and narrower. Spaghetti, bucatini or fettuccine can be used in place of the linguine.

chicken with red pesto pasta

4 chicken breast fillets (1lb 13oz)
¼ cup (2oz) bottled red pesto (*see note, below*)
13oz linguine pasta
1 cup (3oz) stale breadcrumbs
⅓ cup finely chopped fresh chives
2 teaspoons wholegrain mustard
½ cup (125ml) chicken stock

1 Preheat grill.
2 Coat chicken with half the pesto; cook under grill (or on grill plate or barbecue) until browned both sides and cooked through; cover to keep warm.
3 Meanwhile, cook pasta in large saucepan of boiling water until tender; drain. Rinse under cold water; drain.
4 Heat oiled large saucepan; cook breadcrumbs, stirring, until browned. Stir in pasta, remaining pesto, chives, mustard and stock; cook, stirring, until hot.
5 Serve pasta with sliced chicken, and accompany with tomato wedges, if you like.

prep & cook time 30 minutes **serves** 4
nutritional count per serving 14g total fat (3.2g saturated fat); 700 cal; 78.6g carbohydrate; 60.5g protein; 6.1g fiber

We used sun-dried pepper pesto for this recipe, but any bottled 'red' pesto, such as tomato, could be used.

creamy lamb and linguine with mint pesto

1lb 2oz linguine pasta
2 cups firmly packed fresh mint leaves
2 cloves garlic, crushed
⅓ cup (2oz) roasted pine nuts
2 tablespoons coarsely grated Parmesan cheese
⅓ cup (80ml) olive oil
1lb 2oz lamb fillets, sliced thinly
1¼ cups (300ml) cream

1 Cook pasta in large saucepan of boiling water until tender; drain.
2 Meanwhile, process mint, garlic, nuts, cheese and ¼ cup of the oil until combined.
3 Heat remaining oil in medium frying pan; cook lamb, stirring, in batches, until browned.
4 Place mint pesto and cream in same pan; stir well. Add lamb and pasta; stir until hot.

prep & cook time 35 minutes **serves** 4
nutritional count per serving 56.5g total fat
(25.6g saturated fat); 1058 cal; 89.2g carbohydrate;
45.3g protein; 6.8g fiber

linguine with asparagus and chili pancetta

1lb 2oz linguine pasta
5oz thinly sliced chili pancetta, halved
¼ cup (60ml) olive oil
2 cloves garlic, sliced thinly
9oz asparagus, trimmed, sliced thinly
4oz baby rocket leaves
¼ cup (60ml) lemon juice

1 Cook pasta in large saucepan of boiling water until tender; drain. Return pasta to pan.
2 Meanwhile, cook pancetta, in batches, in large frying pan until browned both sides and crisp. Remove from pan; cover to keep warm.
3 Add oil to same pan (there should still be about 1 tablespoon of fat from the pancetta) with garlic and asparagus; cook, stirring, 1 minute or until fragrant.
4 Pour hot asparagus mixture over pasta; add rocket and juice then stir through pancetta.

prep & cook time 35 minutes **serves** 4
nutritional count per serving 20.9g total fat
(4.2g saturated fat); 663 cal; 89.8g carbohydrate;
25.6g protein; 4.8g fiber

linguine with tuna, chili and fresh tomato

13oz linguine pasta
2 x 7oz cans tuna in chili oil
1lb 2oz ripe tomatoes, chopped coarsely
1 fresh large red chili, sliced thinly
¼ cup loosely packed fresh oregano leaves
⅓ cup (80ml) lemon juice
¼ cup (60ml) olive oil

1 Cook pasta in large saucepan of boiling water until tender; drain.
2 Meanwhile, drain tuna, reserving 1 tablespoon of the oil. Place tuna in large bowl; flake with fork.
3 Add pasta to bowl with tomato, chili, oregano, juice, olive oil and reserved chili oil; toss gently.

prep & cook time 20 minutes **serves** 4
nutritional count per serving 8.9g total fat
(1.3g saturated fat); 199 cal; 20g carbohydrate;
9.1g protein; 1.4g fiber

linguine with beans, potatoes and basil pesto

9oz green beans, cut into 2in lengths
2 medium potatoes (14oz), sliced thinly lengthways
1lb 2oz linguine pasta
1¼ cups (4oz) flaked pecorino cheese
basil pesto
1 cup firmly packed fresh basil leaves
¼ cup (1oz) finely grated pecorino cheese
¼ cup (1oz) roasted pine nuts
2 cloves garlic, crushed
½ cup (125ml) olive oil

1 Boil, steam or microwave beans and potato, separately, until just tender; drain.
2 Meanwhile, cook pasta in large saucepan of boiling water, uncovered, until just tender; drain, reserving ½ cup of the cooking liquid.
3 Make basil pesto; stir in reserved cooking liquid.
4 Place beans, potato and pasta in large bowl with pesto and cheese; toss gently.
basil pesto Blend or process ingredients until mixture forms a coarse paste.

prep & cook time 35 minutes **serves** 4
nutritional count per serving 45.3g total fat
(9.9g saturated fat); 925 cal; 101.4g carbohydrate;
27.3g protein; 10.3g fiber

linguine & chorizo in creamy mushroom sauce

11oz Swiss brown mushrooms, halved
2 tablespoons olive oil
2 cloves garlic, crushed
2 chorizo sausages (12oz)
½ cup (125ml) dry white wine
1 cup (250ml) chicken stock
11oz sour cream
4 green onions, chopped finely
13oz linguine pasta
2 tablespoons finely shredded fresh basil

1 Preheat oven to 475°F.
2 Place mushrooms in large shallow baking dish, drizzle with combined oil and garlic; roast, uncovered, about 15 minutes or until mushrooms are browned and tender.
3 Meanwhile, cook chorizo in heated medium frying pan until browned and cooked through; drain on absorbent paper then chop coarsely.
4 Place wine in same cleaned pan; bring to the boil. Reduce heat; simmer, uncovered, 5 minutes. Stir in stock and sour cream; return mixture to the boil. Reduce heat; simmer, uncovered, about 2 minutes or until sauce is hot. Remove from heat; stir in mushrooms and onion.
5 Meanwhile, cook pasta in large saucepan of boiling water until tender; drain. Place pasta in large bowl with mushroom sauce, chorizo and basil; toss gently. Sprinkle with finely grated Parmesan cheese, if you like.

prep & cook time 30 minutes **serves** 4
nutritional count per serving 66g total fat (30.4g saturated fat); 1028 cal; 69.7g carbohydrate; 32.5g protein; 5.8g fiber

chili tuna and lemon linguine

13oz linguine pasta
2 x 3oz cans tuna in oil with chili
2 teaspoons finely grated lemon rind
1 tablespoon lemon juice, approximately
¼ cup coarsely chopped fresh flat-leaf parsley
2 cloves garlic, crushed
¼ cup (60ml) olive oil

1 Cook pasta in large saucepan of boiling water until tender; drain.
2 Place pasta in large bowl with undrained tuna and remaining ingredients; toss gently.

prep & cook time 20 minutes **serves** 4
nutritional count per serving 25.8g total fat (3.8g saturated fat); 579 cal; 64.3g carbohydrate; 20.6g protein; 3.6g fiber

linguine with crab

11oz fresh crab meat
1 clove garlic, crushed
2 fresh small red thai chilies, sliced thinly
½ cup (125ml) dry white wine
1 tablespoon finely grated lemon rind
13oz linguine pasta
½ cup coarsely chopped fresh flat-leaf parsley
1 small red onion (4oz), sliced thinly
⅓ cup (80ml) peanut oil

1 Cook crab, garlic and chili in heated oiled large frying pan, stirring, until crab is just cooked.
2 Add wine and rind to pan; bring to the boil. Reduce heat; simmer, uncovered, until wine reduces by half.
3 Meanwhile, cook pasta in large saucepan of boiling water until tender; drain.
4 Combine pasta in large bowl with crab mixture and remaining ingredients; toss gently.

prep & cook time 25 minutes **serves** 4
nutritional count per serving 19.7g total fat (3.6g saturated fat); 556 cal; 66.5g carbohydrate; 20.6g protein; 4g fiber

crisp-skinned steelhead trout with linguine

13oz linguine pasta
¼ cup (60ml) olive oil
¼ cup loosely packed fresh sage leaves
¼ cup (2oz) rinsed, drained capers
6 green onions, cut into 2in lengths
4 steelhead trout fillets (1lb 15oz), skin on
⅓ cup (80ml) lemon juice
1 tablespoon sweet chili sauce
2 cloves garlic, crushed

1 Cook pasta in large saucepan of boiling water until tender; drain.
2 Meanwhile, heat oil in large frying pan; cook sage, capers and onion, separately, until crisp.
3 Cook fish, skin-side up, on heated oiled grill plate (or grill or barbecue) until crisp both sides and cooked as desired.
4 Place pasta in large bowl with juice, sauce, garlic and half of the sage, half of the capers and half of the onion; toss gently.
5 Divide pasta mixture among serving plates; top with fish, sprinkle with remaining sage, capers and onion.

prep & cook time 30 minutes **serves** 4
nutritional count per serving 18.3g total fat (3g saturated fat); 666 cal; 70g carbohydrate; 53.3g protein; 5.5g fiber

This recipe is good served warm or at room temperature. Assemble the salad just before serving as the pasta will absorb the dressing if not served immediately.

linguine with lamb, asparagus and gremolata

13oz linguine pasta
13oz lamb fillets
1lb 2oz asparagus, trimmed, chopped coarsely
gremolata
⅓ cup finely grated lemon rind
4 cloves garlic, crushed
1 cup coarsely chopped fresh flat-leaf parsley
½ cup (125ml) lemon juice
8 green onions, sliced thinly
1 tablespoon olive oil

1 Cook pasta in large saucepan of boiling water until tender; drain.
2 Meanwhile, cook lamb on heated oiled grill plate (or grill or barbecue) until browned and cooked as desired. Cover, stand 5 minutes then cut into thin slices.
3 Boil, steam or microwave asparagus until tender; drain.
4 Make gremolata.
5 Pour gremolata over pasta. Add lamb and asparagus; toss gently.
gremolata Combine ingredients in small bowl.

prep & cook time 35 minutes **serves** 6
nutritional count per serving 6.2g total fat (1.6g saturated fat); 339 cal; 45.1g carbohydrate; 22.8g protein; 4.3g fiber

chili shrimp linguine

1lb 2oz linguine pasta
⅓ cup (80ml) olive oil
14oz uncooked medium jumbo shrimp, peeled
3 fresh small red thai chilies, chopped finely
2 cloves garlic, crushed
½ cup finely chopped fresh flat-leaf parsley
2 teaspoons finely grated lemon rind

1 Cook pasta in large saucepan of boiling water until tender; drain.
2 Meanwhile, heat oil in large frying pan; cook shrimp, chili and garlic, stirring, until shrimp are just cooked through. Remove from heat; stir in parsley and rind.
3 Combine pasta with shrimp mixture in large bowl; toss gently.

prep & cook time 30 minutes **serves** 4
nutritional count per serving 20.8g total fat (3g saturated fat); 682 cal; 85.5g carbohydrate; 34.7g protein; 4.8g fiber

macaroni

These small, hollow pasta tubes, which can be straight or bent (elbow macaroni), are made with semolina flour and water, but contain no eggs.

macaroni & cheese with olives

13oz macaroni pasta
2oz butter
1 small red onion (4oz), sliced thinly
1 clove garlic, crushed
1 medium red pepper (7oz), sliced thinly
5oz button mushrooms, quartered
⅓ cup (2oz) all-purpose flour
3 cups (750ml) milk
⅓ cup (2oz) tomato paste
⅓ cup (1oz) seeded black olives, halved
½ cup finely chopped fresh basil
1½ cups (5oz) coarsely grated pizza cheese

1 Cook pasta in large saucepan of boiling water until tender; drain.
2 Meanwhile, melt butter in large saucepan; cook onion, garlic, pepper and mushrooms, stirring, until vegetables soften. Add flour; cook, stirring, until mixture bubbles and thickens. Gradually stir in milk. Add paste; cook, stirring, until sauce boils and thickens.
3 Preheat grill.
4 Stir pasta, olives, basil and half the cheese into sauce. Place mixture in deep 8-cup ovenproof dish; sprinkle with remaining cheese. Grill until cheese melts and is browned lightly.

prep & cook time 35 minutes **serves** 4
nutritional count per serving 29.5g total fat (18.4g saturated fat); 771 cal; 90.1g carbohydrate; 32.4g protein; 6.7g fiber

beef, garlic & swiss chard pasta bake

9oz small macaroni pasta
2 teaspoons vegetable oil
4 cloves garlic, crushed
9oz trimmed Swiss chard, sliced thinly
11oz sour cream
5 cups Bolognese sauce (*see note, below*)
½ cup (2oz) coarsely grated cheddar cheese

1 Preheat oven to 400°F.
2 Cook pasta in large saucepan of boiling water until tender; drain. Rinse under cold water; drain.
3 Meanwhile, heat oil in large frying pan; cook garlic, stirring, 1 minute. Add Swiss chard; cook, stirring, until wilted. Stir in pasta and sour cream.
4 Spread half the Bolognese sauce into shallow 12-cup baking dish. Layer with half the Swiss chard mixture; top with remaining sauce then remaining Swiss chard mixture. Sprinkle over cheese.
5 Bake, uncovered, in oven, about 20 minutes or until browned and heated through.

prep & cook time 50 minutes **serves** 6
nutritional count per serving 38.2g total fat (20.5g saturated fat); 635 cal; 38.7g carbohydrate; 31.7g protein; 6g fiber

The Bolognese sauce used for this recipe is from the double amount made for the *spaghetti Bolognese* recipe on page 183. You will need to make that sauce recipe first, to get the amount of Bolognese sauce required for this recipe. Freeze leftover sauce for up to three months.

If you prefer, instead of serving in step 3, place the mixture into a heatproof dish; sprinkle with a little extra cheese then place under a broiler for a few minutes until browned lightly. Or, place the mixture in an ovenproof dish; bake, uncovered, in a moderate oven for about 20 minutes or until browned lightly and heated through.

macaroni & cheese

1 cup (6oz) macaroni pasta
1oz butter
2 tablespoons all-purpose flour
2 teaspoons mustard powder
1½ cups (375ml) milk
¾ cup (3oz) grated cheddar cheese
2 hard-boiled eggs, quartered
½ cup (2oz) frozen peas, thawed
2 tablespoons finely chopped fresh flat-leaf parsley

1 Cook pasta in large saucepan of boiling water until tender; drain.
2 Meanwhile, melt butter in large saucepan, add flour and mustard; cook, stirring constantly, over medium heat, about 2 minutes or until mixture thickens and bubbles, do not allow mixture to brown. Remove from heat; gradually stir in milk. Return to medium heat; stir until sauce boils and thickens slightly. Add cheese; stir until melted.
3 Gently stir pasta, egg, peas and parsley into sauce; serve immediately.

prep & cook time 55 minutes **serves** 4
nutritional count per serving 21.7g total fat (12.3g saturated fat); 441 cal; 40.6g carbohydrate; 19.5g protein; 2.7g fiber

pastitsio

9oz macaroni pasta

2 eggs, beaten lightly

¾ cup (2oz) coarsely grated Parmesan cheese

2 tablespoons stale breadcrumbs

meat sauce

1 tablespoon olive oil

2 medium onions (11oz), chopped finely

1lb 11oz ground beef

14oz can chopped tomatoes

⅓ cup (3oz) tomato paste

½ cup (125ml) beef stock

¼ cup (60ml) dry white wine

½ teaspoon ground cinnamon

1 egg, beaten lightly

cheese topping

3oz butter

½ cup (3oz) all-purpose flour

3½ cups (875ml) milk

1 cup (3oz) coarsely grated Parmesan cheese

2 egg yolks

1 Preheat oven to 350°F. Oil shallow 10-cup ovenproof dish.

2 Make meat sauce. Make cheese topping.

3 Cook pasta in large saucepan of boiling water until tender; drain. Combine warm pasta, egg and cheese in large bowl; mix well. Press pasta over base of dish; top with meat sauce, pour over cheese topping, smooth surface then sprinkle with breadcrumbs.

4 Bake, uncovered, in oven, about 1 hour or until browned lightly. Stand 10 minutes before serving.

meat sauce Heat oil in large saucepan; cook onion, stirring, until soft. Add beef; cook, stirring, until well browned. Stir in undrained tomatoes, paste, stock, wine and cinnamon; simmer, uncovered, until thick. Cool 10 minutes; stir in egg.

cheese topping Melt butter in medium saucepan, add flour; cook, stirring, until mixture thickens and bubbles. Gradually stir in milk; cook, stirring, until sauce boils and thickens. Remove from heat; stir in cheese. Cool 5 minutes; stir in egg yolks.

prep & cook time 2 hours 15 minutes **serves** 6
nutritional count per serving 41.6g total fat (21.8g saturated fat); 822 cal; 54.4g carbohydrate; 54g protein; 3.8g fiber

spicy sausage pasta bake

13oz macaroni pasta
6 thick spicy lamb sausages (2lb)
1 medium onion (5oz), chopped coarsely
1 small eggplant (8oz), chopped coarsely
2 medium red peppers (14oz), chopped coarsely
3 small green zucchini (10oz), chopped coarsely
25oz bottled tomato sauce
½ cup coarsely chopped fresh basil
2 cups (7oz) pizza cheese

1 Preheat oven to 350°F.
2 Cook pasta in large saucepan of boiling water until tender; drain.
3 Meanwhile, cook sausages in heated oiled large frying pan until just cooked through. Drain on absorbent paper.
4 Cook onion, eggplant, peppers and zucchini in same pan, stirring, until just tender.
5 Cut sausages into ¾in slices; add to vegetables in pan with sauce and basil, stir to combine.
6 Combine pasta and sausage mixture in deep 12-cup casserole dish; sprinkle with cheese. Bake, uncovered, in oven, about 20 minutes or until browned lightly.

prep & cook time 50 minutes **serves** 6
nutritional count per serving 36.3g total fat (16.5g saturated fat); 826 cal; 67.7g carbohydrate; 57.6g protein; 7.5g fiber

Try making this recipe with some of the more exotic sausages so readily available these days; one variety with fennel and chili is especially delicious when cooked in tomato sauce.

macaroni with beef sausages

14oz thin beef sausages
2½ cups (600ml) bottled tomato sauce
4 stalks celery (1lb 5oz), trimmed, chopped coarsely
1 medium green pepper (7oz), chopped coarsely
9oz elbow macaroni pasta
2 tablespoons finely chopped fresh basil
1 cup (4oz) grated mozzarella cheese

1 Cook sausages, in batches, in heated oiled large frying pan until browned all over and cooked through; drain on absorbent paper. Cut sausages into ½in slices.
2 Place sauce in same cleaned pan; bring to the boil. Add sausage, celery and pepper; cook, stirring occasionally, about 5 minutes or until vegetables are just tender.
3 Meanwhile, cook pasta in large saucepan of boiling water until tender; drain.
4 Combine pasta, basil and cheese in pan with sausage and tomato sauce; toss gently.

prep & cook time 30 minutes **serves** 4
nutritional count per serving 33g total fat
(16g saturated fat); 685 cal; 63.4g carbohydrate;
28.8g protein; 10g fiber

bacon and cheese macaroni

13oz macaroni pasta
1lb 2oz broccoli, trimmed, chopped finely
1 tablespoon olive oil
1 medium onion (5oz), chopped finely
9oz bacon, sliced thinly
2 cloves garlic, crushed
1¼ cups (300ml) cream
1 cup (3oz) grated Parmesan cheese
½ cup (2oz) grated cheddar cheese

1 Cook pasta in large saucepan of boiling water until tender. Add broccoli 1 minute before end of cooking time; drain. Return to pan; cover to keep warm.
2 Meanwhile, heat oil in large frying pan; cook onion, bacon and garlic, stirring, until bacon is crisp. Add cream, cook, stirring, until sauce thickens slightly, stir in half the Parmesan.
3 Preheat grill.
4 Add sauce to pasta, stir to combine. Spoon mixture into an oiled 8-cup ovenproof dish. Top with combined remaining Parmesan and cheddar. Grill until cheese is browned lightly.

prep & cook time 25 minutes **serves** 4
nutritional count per serving 51.9g total fat (30.4g saturated fat); 898 cal; 68.9g carbohydrate; 35.8g protein; 7.3g fiber

baked three cheese pasta

13oz macaroni pasta
1¼ cups (300ml) cream
⅓ cup (80ml) vegetable stock
1¼ cups (5oz) grated fontina cheese
⅓ cup (3oz) crumbled gorgonzola cheese
1¼ cups (4oz) grated Parmesan cheese
1 teaspoon Dijon mustard
2 tablespoons finely chopped fresh flat-leaf parsley
1 tablespoon finely chopped fresh chives

1 Preheat oven to 400°F.
2 Cook pasta in large saucepan of boiling water until tender; drain.
3 Heat cream and stock in medium saucepan until hot. Remove pan from heat, add fontina, gorgonzola and half the Parmesan; stir until melted. Add mustard and herbs. Combine cream mixture with pasta.
4 Pour pasta mixture into 10-cup ovenproof dish. Top with remaining Parmesan. Bake, uncovered, in oven, 15 minutes or until browned lightly.

prep & cook time 35 minutes **serves** 4
nutritional count per serving 59.2g total fat (38g saturated fat); 937 cal; 66.4g carbohydrate; 35.4g protein; 3.3g fiber

pappardelle

Pappardelle is the widest ribbon pasta available; it can have scalloped or straight sides, and is sometimes sold as lasagnatte or even lasagna. Any long pasta such as fettuccine or tagliatelle can be substituted.

pappardelle with chili & semi-dried tomato sauce

2 medium onions (11oz), chopped coarsely
2 cloves garlic, quartered
1 cup (5oz) semi-dried tomatoes in oil, drained
¼ cup (3oz) tomato paste
2 fresh small red thai chilies, chopped finely
2 cups (500ml) beef stock (*see note, below*)
13oz pappardelle pasta
¼ cup coarsely chopped fresh flat-leaf parsley

1 Blend or process onion, garlic, tomatoes, paste and chili until mixture forms a paste.
2 Heat oiled large frying pan; cook tomato mixture, stirring, 10 minutes. Stir in stock; bring to the boil. Reduce heat; simmer sauce, uncovered, about 10 minutes or until thickened slightly.
3 Meanwhile, cook pasta in large saucepan of boiling water until tender; drain.
4 Gently toss pasta through sauce; sprinkle with parsley.

prep & cook time 40 minutes **serves** 6
nutritional count per serving 2.9g total fat (0.4g saturated fat); 314 cal; 55.7g carbohydrate; 11.9g protein; 7g fiber

To make this a meal suitable for vegetarians, substitute vegetable stock for the beef stock.

To make this a meal suitable for vegetarians, substitute vegetable stock for the chicken stock.

pappardelle with roasted mushrooms & tomato

7oz flat mushrooms, quartered
7oz button mushrooms, halved
7oz Swiss brown mushrooms, halved
9oz cherry tomatoes
½ cup (125ml) chicken stock (*see note, above*)
2 teaspoons garlic salt
13oz pappardelle or fettuccine pasta
¼ cup torn fresh basil leaves
¼ cup (1oz) shaved Parmesan cheese

1 Preheat oven to 425°F.
2 Combine mushrooms, tomatoes and stock in baking dish; sprinkle with salt. Bake, uncovered, about 20 minutes or until mushrooms are tender and tomatoes softened.
3 Meanwhile, cook pasta in large pan of boiling water until just tender; drain.
4 Gently toss mushroom mixture through pasta; sprinkle with basil and cheese.

prep & cook time 30 minutes **serves** 4
nutritional count per serving 3.3g total fat
(1.3g saturated fat); 387 cal; 66g carbohydrate;
18.5g protein; 7.9g fiber

pappardelle with lobster

8lbs 1oz uncooked lobster
1 tablespoon finely grated lemon rind
⅓ cup (80ml) lemon juice
1 teaspoon Dijon mustard
1 tablespoon olive oil
13oz pappardelle pasta
½ cup coarsely chopped fresh basil
½ cup coarsely chopped fresh flat-leaf parsley
4 green onions, sliced thinly

1 Place lobster upside-down on chopping board; cut tail from body, discard body. Halve tail lengthways; discard back vein.
2 Combine rind, juice, mustard and oil in large bowl.
3 Cook pasta in large saucepan of boiling water until just tender; drain.
4 Meanwhile, cook lobster, in batches, on heated lightly oiled grill plate (or grill or barbecue) until just changed in color.
5 Add pasta and lobster to rind mixture in bowl with herbs and onion; toss gently to combine.

prep & cook time 35 minutes **serves** 4
nutritional count per serving 8.5g total fat
(1.5g saturated fat); 643 cal; 66.9g carbohydrate;
71.8g protein; 2.8g fiber

roasted pumpkin, sage and garlic pappardelle

2lb 4oz pumpkin, diced into 1in pieces
4 cloves garlic, unpeeled
cooking-oil spray
1lb 2oz pappardelle pasta
1 cup (250ml) vegetable stock
1½ cups (375ml) can light evaporated milk
1 teaspoon olive oil
⅓ cup loosely packed fresh sage leaves
⅓ cup (1oz) finely grated Parmesan cheese

1 Preheat oven to 425°F. Lightly oil oven tray.
2 Place pumpkin and garlic on tray; spray lightly with oil. Roast, uncovered, about 40 minutes or until pumpkin and garlic are tender. When cool enough to handle, peel garlic.
3 Meanwhile, cook pasta in large saucepan of boiling water until tender, drain.
4 Blend or process pumpkin and garlic with stock and milk until smooth.
5 Heat oil in medium saucepan; cook sage, stirring, until crisp, remove from pan.
6 Add pumpkin sauce to pan; stir until heated through. Stir in half the cheese.
7 Return pasta to large saucepan with pumpkin sauce, toss gently. Divide pasta among serving bowls; sprinkle with sage and remaining cheese.

prep & cook time 1 hour 10 minutes **serves** 4
nutritional count per serving 6.7g total fat (2.7g saturated fat); 622 cal; 109.8g carbohydrate; 29.4g protein; 7.1g fiber

clear shrimp & crushed noodle soup

1lb 2oz uncooked medium jumbo shrimp
5oz pappardelle or fettuccine pasta, broken roughly
1.25 liters (5 cups) chicken stock
2 cups (500ml) water
1oz piece fresh galangal, chopped finely
1½in piece fresh ginger (1oz), chopped finely
4 kaffir lime leaves
4in stick fresh lemon grass (1oz), finely chopped
⅓ cup (80ml) lemon juice
¼ cup (60ml) fish sauce
1 tablespoon sambal oelek
1 fresh small red thai chili, sliced thinly
¼ cup coarsely chopped fresh coriander

1 Shell and devein shrimp, leaving tails intact.
2 Cook pasta in large saucepan of boiling water until tender; drain.
3 Meanwhile, combine stock, the water, galangal, ginger, lime leaves and lemon grass in large saucepan; bring to the boil. Boil, uncovered, about 5 minutes or until reduced by a quarter. Add juice, sauce, sambal and shrimp, reduce heat; cook, uncovered, until shrimp just change in color. Remove from heat; discard lime leaves, add chili and coriander.
4 Divide pasta and shrimp mixture among serving bowls; ladle soup over the top.

prep & cook time 25 minutes **serves** 4
nutritional count per serving 2.3g total fat (0.8g saturated fat); 236 cal; 30.5g carbohydrate; 22.1g protein; 1.8g fiber

Be sure not to overcook the chicken livers or they will be dry and unappealing.

chicken liver sauce with pappardelle

1lb 2oz chicken livers, trimmed
½ cup (2oz) packaged breadcrumbs
¼ cup (60ml) olive oil
1 medium onion (5oz), chopped coarsely
4 medium tomatoes (1lb 5oz), chopped coarsely
½ cup (125ml) chicken stock
¼ cup (60ml) balsamic vinegar
¼ cup (60ml) dry red wine
2 tablespoons coarsely chopped fresh rosemary
13oz pappardelle pasta or curly lasagna sliced thickly

1 Halve livers; toss in breadcrumbs, shake off excess. Heat half of the oil in large frying pan; cook liver over high heat, in batches, until browned and cooked (*see note, above*).
2 Heat remaining oil in same pan; cook onion, stirring, until soft. Add tomato; cook, stirring, until tomato is pulpy. Add stock, vinegar, wine and rosemary to the pan; cook, stirring, until sauce thickens slightly.
3 Meanwhile, cook pasta in large saucepan of boiling water until tender; drain.
4 Stir pasta and liver into tomato sauce; toss gently.

prep & cook time 30 minutes **serves** 4
nutritional count per serving 20.3g total fat (3.9g saturated fat); 670 cal; 78.6g carbohydrate; 37.1g protein; 5.9g fiber

pappardelle chicken and creamy mushroom sauce

2 tablespoons olive oil
1 clove garlic, crushed
1 small onion (3oz), chopped finely
9oz Swiss brown mushrooms, sliced thinly
¾ cup (180ml) cream
2 teaspoons finely chopped fresh rosemary
1oz butter
1lb 2oz pappardelle pasta
3 cups (1lb 1oz) shredded cooked chicken
½ cup (2oz) coarsely chopped roasted walnuts
¼ cup coarsely chopped fresh flat-leaf parsley
¾ cup (2oz) grated Parmesan cheese

1 Heat oil in large frying pan; cook garlic and onion, stirring, until onion softens. Add mushrooms; cook, stirring, until just tender.
2 Add cream and rosemary to pan; bring to the boil. Reduce heat, simmer, uncovered, until sauce thickens slightly. Add butter; stir until butter melts.
3 Meanwhile, cook pasta in large saucepan of boiling water until tender; drain. Return to pan.
4 Add cream sauce, chicken, nuts, parsley and half the cheese to pasta; toss gently. Serve sprinkled with remaining cheese.

prep & cook time 30 minutes **serves** 4
nutritional count per serving 55.7g total fat (21.5g saturated fat); 1088 cal; 91.5g carbohydrate; 54.9g protein; 9.3g fiber

You will need to buy a barbecued chicken weighing about 2lb for this recipe. Discard skin and bones before shredding the chicken meat.

The pepper mixture can be made several hours ahead; reheat and complete recipe just before serving.

ricotta, red pepper and chili pappardelle

¼ cup (60ml) olive oil
2 cloves garlic, crushed
½ teaspoon dried chili flakes
4 large red peppers (3lb 6oz), sliced thinly
¼ cup (60ml) water
13oz pappardelle pasta
¼ cup finely chopped fresh chives
2 cups (14oz) firm ricotta cheese
½ cup (4oz) firm ricotta cheese, sliced, extra

1   Heat oil in large saucepan, add garlic and chili; cook, stirring, until fragrant. Add peppers and water; simmer, covered, 15 minutes or until pepper is soft.
2   Meanwhile, cook pasta in large saucepan of boiling water until tender; drain.
3   Add pasta and chives to pepper mixture. Break ricotta into large pieces, add to pan; toss gently.
4   Serve pasta topped with extra ricotta. If you like, sprinkle with extra dried chili and drizzle with a little extra olive oil before serving.

prep & cook time 30 minutes **serves** 4
nutritional count per serving 29.3g total fat (11.1g saturated fat); 686 cal; 74.9g carbohydrate; 27.5g protein; 6.1g fiber

pappardelle with roasted tomato, spinach and ricotta

¼ cup (60ml) balsamic vinegar
3 cloves garlic, crushed
4 medium tomatoes (1lb 5oz), cut into eight wedges
13oz pappardelle pasta
4oz baby spinach leaves
2 tablespoons olive oil
7oz firm ricotta cheese

1 Preheat oven to 400°F.
2 Combine vinegar and garlic in small jug. Place tomato, in single layer, on oven tray; pour vinegar mixture over tomato. Roast, uncovered, about 25 minutes or until tomato is browned lightly and softened.
3 Meanwhile, cook pasta in large saucepan of boiling water until tender; drain.
4 Place pasta, tomato, spinach and oil in large bowl. Break ricotta into about 1¼in pieces; add to pasta mixture, toss gently to combine.

prep & cook time 35 minutes **serves** 4
nutritional count per serving 15.9g total fat (5.1g saturated fat); 479 cal; 64.9g carbohydrate; 16.5g protein; 4.1g fiber

penne

This cylinder shaped pasta, named after a pen or quill because of its shape, can be smooth (lisce) or ridged (rigate). It is a perennial favorite as the hollow center allows it to hold more sauce.

baked penne with peas, mushrooms & leek

14oz penne pasta
2 tablespoons vegetable oil
2oz butter
1 clove garlic, crushed
2 small leeks (14oz), sliced thinly
11oz button mushrooms, quartered
⅓ cup finely chopped fresh chives
2 cups (9oz) frozen peas, thawed
béchamel sauce
4oz butter
⅔ cup (4oz) all-purpose flour
5 cups hot milk
2½ cups (11oz) coarsely grated cheddar cheese

1 Cook pasta in large saucepan of boiling water until tender; drain.
2 Meanwhile, make béchamel sauce.
3 Preheat oven to 350°F.
4 Heat oil and butter in medium frying pan; cook garlic, leek and mushrooms, stirring, until leek softens.
5 Combine pasta and leek mixture in large bowl with chives and peas. Reserve ⅔ cup béchamel sauce for top. Stir remaining sauce into leek mixture. Spoon leek mixture into 15-cup ovenproof dish; spread with reserved béchamel sauce.
6 Bake, uncovered, in oven, about 40 minutes or until browned lightly. Serve with a leafy salad, if you like.
béchamel sauce Melt butter in medium saucepan, add flour; cook, stirring, until mixture thickens and bubbles. Gradually stir in milk; stir until sauce boils and thickens. Remove from heat; stir in cheese.

prep & cook time 1 hour 25 minutes **serves** 6
nutritional count per serving 53.1g total fat (30.6g saturated fat); 915 cal; 71.9g carbohydrate; 34.2g protein; 7.7g fiber

penne with cherry tomatoes and salami

1lb 2oz penne pasta
5oz sliced hot salami
1lb 2oz cherry tomatoes
2 cloves garlic, crushed
⅓ cup loosely packed fresh flat-leaf parsley leaves
¼ cup loosely packed fresh oregano leaves
7oz baby bocconcini cheese, halved
2 tablespoons olive oil

1 Cook pasta in large saucepan of boiling water until tender; drain.
2 Meanwhile, cook salami in large frying pan, stirring, until crisp; drain on absorbent paper.
3 Cook tomatoes in same pan, stirring, until softened. Add garlic; cook, stirring, until fragrant.
4 Place hot pasta, salami and tomato mixture in large bowl with herbs, cheese and oil; toss gently.

prep & cook time 30 minutes **serves** 4
nutritional count per serving 32.4g total fat (11.2g saturated fat); 787 cal; 88.7g carbohydrate; 31.6g protein; 6.6g fiber

penne with amatriciana sauce

1 tablespoon olive oil
1 medium onion (5oz), chopped finely
13oz bacon, sliced thinly
2 large tomatoes (1lb 2oz), peeled, chopped coarsely
1 fresh small red thai chili, chopped finely
13oz penne pasta

1 Heat oil in large frying pan; cook onion and bacon, stirring, about 5 minutes or until onion is soft. Drain away excess fat. Stir in tomato and chili; simmer, uncovered, 5 minutes, stirring occasionally.
2 Meanwhile, cook pasta in large saucepan of boiling water until tender; drain.
3 Combine sauce and pasta.

prep & cook time 30 minutes **serves** 4
nutritional count per serving 8.8g total fat (1.9g saturated fat); 464 cal; 68.6g carbohydrate; 24.1g protein; 5.1g fiber

Pancetta can be substituted for bacon in this recipe.

chicken penne with mushroom sauce

13oz penne pasta
2 teaspoons olive oil
1lb 11oz chicken breast fillets, chopped coarsely
9oz button mushrooms, sliced thinly
½ cup (125ml) dry white wine
⅓ cup (80ml) tomato juice
3 green onions, sliced thickly
2 small tomatoes (4oz), seeded, sliced thinly

1 Cook pasta in large saucepan of boiling water until tender; drain.
2 Meanwhile, heat oil in large frying pan; cook chicken, in batches, until chicken is browned all over.
3 Cook mushrooms in same pan; stirring, until tender. Add wine; bring to the boil. Reduce heat, simmer, uncovered, 2 minutes. Return chicken to pan with juice, onion and tomato; simmer, uncovered, until sauce thickens slightly and chicken is cooked through.
4 Serve pasta topped with chicken and mushroom sauce.

prep & cook time 30 minutes **serves** 4
nutritional count per serving 7.8g total fat
(1.6g saturated fat); 592 cal; 65.7g carbohydrate;
55.6g protein; 5.1g fiber

blue cheese penne and tomatoes

6 small tomatoes (13oz), halved
1 tablespoon olive oil
11oz penne pasta
4oz blue cheese, crumbled
4oz tub light cream cheese, softened
1 cup (3oz) finely grated Parmesan cheese
7oz baby spinach leaves

1 Preheat grill.
2 Place tomatoes, cut-side up, on grill tray; drizzle with oil. Place under grill about 10 minutes or until soft and browned lightly; cover to keep warm.
3 Meanwhile, cook pasta in large saucepan of boiling water until tender. Drain; return pasta to pan.
4 Add blue cheese, cream cheese, half the Parmesan and spinach to hot pasta; toss until well combined.
5 Place pasta mixture in shallow 10-cup ovenproof dish; sprinkle with remaining Parmesan. Cook under grill until top is golden brown. Serve with tomatoes.

prep & cook time 35 minutes **serves** 4
nutritional count per serving 27.4g total fat
(14.8g saturated fat); 582 cal; 54.2g carbohydrate;
27.1g protein; 4.9g fiber

Be careful not to have heat too high when whisking egg yolks with the vinegar mixture, or you'll end up with scrambled eggs rather than a smooth hollandaise.

penne, parmesan and asparagus hollandaise

¼ cup (60ml) white vinegar
1 tablespoon coarsely chopped fresh tarragon leaves
8 whole black peppercorns
4 egg yolks
9oz cold unsalted butter, chopped
1 tablespoon lemon juice
13oz penne pasta
2lb 4oz asparagus, trimmed, chopped coarsely
⅓ cup (1oz) grated Parmesan cheese

1 Combine vinegar, tarragon and peppercorns in small saucepan; bring to the boil. Reduce heat, simmer, uncovered, until mixture reduces to about 1 tablespoon. Strain vinegar mixture into large heatproof bowl, discard tarragon and peppercorns.
2 Place bowl containing vinegar mixture over large saucepan of simmering water; whisk in egg yolks until mixture is light and fluffy. Gradually add butter, whisking continuously between additions until hollandaise sauce thickens; stir in juice.
3 Cook pasta in large saucepan of boiling water until tender; drain.
4 Meanwhile, boil, steam or microwave asparagus until just tender; drain.
5 Place pasta, asparagus, cheese and hollandaise sauce in large bowl; toss gently to combine.

prep & cook time 35 minutes **serves** 4
nutritional count per serving 60.9g total fat (37.4g saturated fat); 905 cal; 66.9g carbohydrate; 20.7g protein; 5.6g fiber

penne with lamb and roasted pepper

3 large red peppers (2lb 4oz)
1lb 2oz lamb fillets
2 tablespoons olive oil
2 teaspoons ground cumin
2 x 15oz cans tomato puree
½ cup (2oz) drained semi-dried tomatoes,
    chopped coarsely
13oz penne pasta
¼ cup finely shredded fresh basil

1 Quarter peppers, remove seeds and membranes. Roast pepper, skin-side up, under very hot grill until skin blisters and blackens. Cover pepper with plastic or paper for 5 minutes; peel away skin, then slice pepper thinly.
2 Combine lamb, oil and cumin in medium bowl. Cook lamb, in batches, in heated oiled large frying pan (or grill or barbecue) until browned all over and cooked as desired. Stand 5 minutes; cut into thin slices.
3 Heat large frying pan, add puree, tomato and pepper; bring to the boil. Reduce heat, simmer, uncovered, about 5 minutes or until sauce thickens slightly.
4 Meanwhile, cook pasta in large saucepan of boiling water until tender; drain.
5 Place pasta in large bowl with lamb, tomato sauce and basil; toss gently to combine.

prep & cook time 25 minutes **serves** 4
nutritional count per serving 15.9g total fat (3.6g saturated fat); 709 cal; 88.4g carbohydrate; 45.9g protein; 11.7g fiber

penne primavera

13oz penne pasta

1 tablespoon olive oil

1 large onion (7oz), chopped finely

2 cloves garlic, crushed

4 baby carrots (2oz), chopped finely

5oz green beans, chopped finely

4oz snow peas, trimmed, halved

9oz asparagus, chopped coarsely

1 tablespoon fresh oregano leaves

2 teaspoons fresh thyme leaves

14oz can diced tomatoes

1¼ cups (4oz) shaved Parmesan cheese

1 Cook pasta in large saucepan of boiling water until tender; drain.

2 Meanwhile, heat oil in large frying pan. Cook onion, stirring occasionally, over low heat, until very soft but not browned. Add garlic and carrot; cook 1 minute.

3 Stir in beans; cook until changed in color. Stir in snow peas and asparagus; cook until changed in color. Add herbs and tomato; bring to the boil. Reduce heat; simmer until heated through and thickened slightly.

4 Toss pasta through hot sauce; serve with cheese.

prep & cook time 50 minutes **serves** 4
nutritional count per serving 14.5g total fat
(6.1g saturated fat); 552 cal; 75.1g carbohydrate;
25.8g protein; 7.1g fiber

penne chili con carne

13oz penne pasta
1 tablespoon peanut oil
1 large onion (7oz), sliced thinly
2 cloves garlic, crushed
2 fresh small red thai chilies, chopped coarsely
1 teaspoon ground cumin
1 teaspoon ground coriander
13oz yellow cherry tomatoes, halved
1lb 2oz thinly sliced cooked roast beef
15oz can kidney beans, rinsed, drained
2⅓ cups (21oz) bottled tomato sauce
⅓ cup loosely packed fresh coriander leaves

1   Cook pasta in large saucepan of boiling water until tender; drain.
2   Meanwhile, heat oil in large saucepan; cook onion, garlic, chili and ground spices, stirring, until onion softens. Add tomato; cook, stirring, until tomato is just soft. Add beef, beans and sauce; bring to the boil. Simmer, uncovered, until sauce thickens slightly.
3   Add pasta to pan; toss gently over heat until hot. Stir in fresh coriander.

prep & cook time 30 minutes **serves** 4
nutritional count per serving 12.9g total fat (3.9g saturated fat); 723 cal; 93.1g carbohydrate; 50.8g protein; 12.8g fiber

pepper-crusted lamb fillet with penne in red pepper sauce

3 medium red peppers (1lb 5oz)

1lb 5oz lamb fillets

1 tablespoon cracked black pepper

1 tablespoon olive oil

1 medium onion (5oz), chopped finely

2 cloves garlic, crushed

1¼ cups (300ml) cream

13oz penne pasta

⅔ cup coarsely chopped fresh basil

1 Quarter peppers; discard seeds and membranes. Roast, skin-side up, under very hot grill until skin blisters and blackens. Cover pepper in plastic or paper for 5 minutes; peel away skin then chop pepper coarsely.

2 Combine lamb and pepper in medium bowl; cook lamb, in batches, in heated oiled large frying pan until browned all over and cooked as desired. Cover lamb; stand 5 minutes then slice thinly.

3 Heat oil in same pan; cook onion and garlic, stirring, until onion softens. Add cream; bring to the boil. Remove from heat; blend or process cream mixture with pepper until mixture is smooth.

4 Meanwhile, cook pasta in large saucepan of boiling water until tender; drain.

5 Place pasta in large bowl with lamb, sauce and basil; toss gently.

prep & cook time 35 minutes **serves** 4
nutritional count per serving 51.9g total fat (28.5g saturated fat); 944 cal; 73.3g carbohydrate; 46.3g protein; 6.1g fiber

penne with tomato salsa and tuna

13oz penne pasta
3 medium tomatoes (1lb 4oz), chopped finely
1 medium red onion (6oz), chopped finely
2 cloves garlic, crushed
¼ cup firmly packed, torn fresh basil leaves
15oz can tuna in brine, drained, flaked
¼ cup (60ml) balsamic vinegar

1 Cook pasta in large saucepan of boiling water until tender; drain.
2 Place pasta in large bowl with remaining ingredients; toss gently.

prep & cook time 35 minutes **serves** 4
nutritional count per serving 3.4g total fat (1.1g saturated fat); 448 cal; 67.5g carbohydrate; 33.1g protein; 4.7g fiber

pasta with creamy bacon sauce

1lb 2oz penne pasta
1 tablespoon olive oil
1 large leek (1lb 2oz), sliced thinly
9oz bacon, chopped coarsely
1 clove garlic, crushed
2 large zucchini (11oz), sliced thinly
13oz button mushrooms, halved
2 tablespoons Dijon mustard
1¼ cups (11oz) light sour cream
¾ cup (180ml) milk

1 Cook pasta in large saucepan of boiling water until tender; drain.
2 Meanwhile, heat oil in large frying pan, add leek, bacon and garlic; cook, stirring, until leek is soft and bacon is browned lightly.
3 Add zucchini and mushrooms to pan; cook, stirring, until zucchini is just tender. Stir in mustard, sour cream and milk; cook, stirring, until hot. Toss sauce through pasta.

prep & cook time 25 minutes **serves** 4
nutritional count per serving 28.3g total fat (13.6g saturated fat); 786 cal; 95.8g carbohydrate; 31.3g protein; 10.1g fiber

penne puttanesca

1lb 2oz penne pasta
⅓ cup (80ml) olive oil
3 cloves garlic, crushed
1 teaspoon dried chili flakes
5 medium tomatoes (2lb 2oz), chopped coarsely
1¼ cups (7oz) seeded kalamata olives
8 anchovy fillets, drained, chopped coarsely
⅓ cup (2oz) rinsed drained capers
⅓ cup coarsely chopped fresh flat-leaf parsley
2 tablespoons finely shredded fresh basil

1 Cook pasta in large saucepan of boiling water until tender; drain.
2 Meanwhile, heat oil in large frying pan; cook garlic, stirring, until fragrant. Add chili and tomato; cook, stirring, 5 minutes. Add remaining ingredients; cook, stirring, about 5 minutes or until sauce thickens slightly.
3 Add pasta to puttanesca sauce; toss gently to combine.

prep & cook time 25 minutes **serves** 4
nutritional count per serving 20.9g total fat (3g saturated fat); 695 cal; 102.6g carbohydrate; 19.1g protein; 8.5g fiber

tuna and artichoke pasta

1lb 2oz penne pasta
1 medium lemon (5oz)
¼ cup (60ml) olive oil
4 medium tomatoes (1lb 11oz), chopped coarsely
2 cloves garlic, crushed
15oz can tuna in oil, undrained, flaked
2 x 10oz jars marinated artichoke hearts, drained
½ cup coarsely chopped fresh flat-leaf parsley

1 Cook pasta in large saucepan of boiling water until tender; drain.
2 Meanwhile, peel rind thinly from lemon, avoiding any white pith. Cut rind into thin strips; reserve. Squeeze juice from lemon (you need 2 tablespoons of juice).
3 Heat 1 tablespoon of the oil in large frying pan; cook tomato and garlic, stirring, until tomato has softened. Add tuna, juice, artichokes and remaining oil; stir until heated through. Stir in parsley.
4 Toss pasta with sauce. Divide among serving bowls; sprinkle with reserved rind.

prep & cook time 30 minutes **serves** 4
nutritional count per serving 30.1g total fat (4.5g saturated fat); 832 cal; 90.5g carbohydrate; 44g protein; 9.8g fiber

penne, roast pepper and baby vegetables in burnt butter sauce

2 medium red peppers (14oz)
13oz penne pasta
7oz baby corn, halved lengthways
7oz green beans, trimmed
4oz butter
2 cloves garlic, crushed
2 tablespoons coarsely chopped fresh oregano

1 Quarter peppers; discard seeds and membranes. Roast under hot grill, skin-side up, until skin blisters and blackens. Cover pepper with plastic or paper for 5 minutes; peel away skin then slice pepper thinly.
2 Meanwhile, cook pasta in large saucepan of boiling water until tender; drain.
3 Boil, steam or microwave corn and beans, separately, until just tender; drain.
4 Melt butter in small saucepan; cook, stirring, about 3 minutes or until browned. Remove from heat; stir in garlic and oregano.
5 Place pepper, pasta, corn and beans in large bowl with burnt butter mixture; toss gently.

prep & cook time 35 minutes **serves** 4
nutritional count per serving 22.4g total fat (13.7g saturated fat); 588 cal; 77g carbohydrate; 15.3g protein; 7.9g fiber

penne with char-grilled pepper and pine nuts

2 large red peppers (1lb 9oz)
13oz penne pasta
2 tablespoons olive oil
2 cloves garlic, crushed
½ cup (3oz) roasted pine nuts
2 fresh small red thai chilies, chopped finely
¼ cup (60ml) lemon juice
4oz baby rocket leaves
4oz feta cheese, crumbled

1 Quarter peppers; discard seeds and membranes. Roast under hot grill, skin-side up, until skin blisters and blackens. Cover pepper with plastic or paper for 5 minutes; peel away skin then slice pepper thinly.
2 Meanwhile, cook pasta in large saucepan of boiling water until tender; drain.
3 Heat oil in large frying pan; cook garlic, nuts and chili, stirring, about 2 minutes or until fragrant. Add pepper and juice; stir until hot.
4 Place pasta and pepper mixture in large bowl with rocket and cheese; toss gently to combine.

prep & cook time 35 minutes **serves** 4
nutritional count per serving 30.5g total fat (6.2g saturated fat); 659 cal; 74.4g carbohydrate; 21g protein; 8.2g fiber

penne bolognese

2 tablespoons olive oil
1 small onion (3oz), chopped finely
1 medium carrot (4oz), chopped finely
1 stalk celery (5oz), trimmed, chopped finely
2 cloves garlic, sliced thinly
1lb 2oz ground beef
1lb 2oz ground pork
½ cup (125ml) milk
½ cup (125ml) dry white wine
2 x 14oz cans crushed tomatoes
1 cup (250ml) beef stock
1lb 2oz penne pasta

1 Heat oil in large saucepan, add onion, carrot, celery and garlic; cook, stirring, until celery softens. Add minces; cook, stirring, until browned. Add milk and wine; simmer, uncovered, until liquid is almost evaporated. Add undrained tomatoes; cook, stirring, 5 minutes. Add stock; bring to the boil. Reduce heat; simmer, covered, 30 minutes.
2 Cook pasta in large saucepan of boiling water until tender; drain. Serve sauce with pasta; sprinkle with finely grated Parmesan cheese, if you like.

prep & cook time 1 hour 15 minutes **serves** 6
nutritional count per serving 19.8g total fat (6.2g saturated fat); 646 cal; 64.4g carbohydrate; 45.7g protein; 5.6g fiber

fresh tomato and chili pasta

1lb 2oz penne pasta
⅓ cup (80ml) olive oil
1 clove garlic, crushed
1 fresh small red thai chili, chopped finely
4 medium ripe tomatoes (1lb 13oz), chopped coarsely
1 cup coarsely chopped fresh flat-leaf parsley
½ cup (1oz) Parmesan cheese flakes

1 Cook pasta in large saucepan of boiling water until tender; drain.
2 Meanwhile, heat oil in large frying pan, add garlic and chili; cook, stirring, about 1 minute or until fragrant. Stir in tomato and parsley; remove from heat.
3 Add sauce mixture to pasta; toss gently. Serve topped with cheese.

prep & cook time 20 minutes **serves** 4
nutritional count per serving 23.1g total fat (4.9g saturated fat); 662 cal; 89.2g carbohydrate; 20.2g protein; 7.4g fiber

roasted tomato with basil and olive oil

8 medium tomatoes (1lb 5oz), quartered
2 cloves garlic, crushed
¼ cup (60ml) olive oil
1lb 2oz penne pasta
1 cup loosely packed fresh basil leaves

1 Preheat oven to 425°F.
2 Combine tomato, garlic and oil in large baking dish; roast, uncovered, about 15 minutes or until tomato softens and browns slightly.
3 Meanwhile, cook pasta in large saucepan of boiling water until tender; drain.
4 Place tomato mixture and pasta in large bowl with basil; toss gently.

prep & cook time 30 minutes **serves** 4
nutritional count per serving 15.2g total fat (2.2g saturated fat); 569 cal; 88.3g carbohydrate; 15.7g protein; 6.3g fiber

bacon, zucchini and basil pasta

13oz penne pasta
1 tablespoon olive oil
9oz bacon, sliced thinly
3 medium zucchini (9oz), sliced thinly
2 cloves garlic, crushed
2 small tomatoes (6oz), seeded, sliced thinly
⅓ cup (3oz) crème fraîche
¼ cup small fresh basil leaves
⅓ cup (1oz) Parmesan cheese flakes

1 Cook pasta in large saucepan of boiling water until tender; drain.
2 Meanwhile, heat oil in large frying pan; cook bacon and zucchini, stirring, until bacon is crisp and zucchini is browned lightly. Add garlic; cook, stirring, until fragrant.
3 Combine pasta and bacon mixture with tomato and crème fraîche; stir in basil leaves. Serve topped with cheese.

prep & cook time 30 minutes **serves** 4
nutritional count per serving 18.8g total fat (8.7g saturated fat); 535 cal; 66.2g carbohydrate; 22.3g protein; 4.6g fiber

fresh tomato and caper salsa with penne

13oz penne pasta
6 medium tomatoes (2lb), seeded, chopped finely
⅓ cup (3oz) rinsed, drained capers, chopped coarsely
1 medium red onion (6oz), chopped finely
12 basil leaves, torn
12 purple basil leaves, torn
½ cup (3oz) roasted pine nuts
balsamic vinaigrette
2 cloves garlic, crushed
⅓ cup (80ml) balsamic vinegar
⅔ cup (160ml) olive oil

1 Cook pasta in large saucepan of boiling water until tender; drain.
2 Meanwhile, make balsamic vinaigrette.
3 Place pasta in large bowl with remaining ingredients; drizzle with vinaigrette, toss gently.
balsamic vinaigrette Combine ingredients in screw-top jar; shake well.

prep & cook time 25 minutes **serves** 4
nutritional count per serving 51.7g total fat (6.2g saturated fat); 819 cal; 71g carbohydrate; 15g protein; 6.6g fiber

Place leftover pasta and sauce in an oiled ovenproof dish, cover with mozzarella and bake in a moderate oven until heated through and cheese bubbles.

penne arrabiata

1 tablespoon olive oil
2 medium onions (11oz), chopped finely
5 cloves garlic, crushed
3 fresh small red thai chilies, chopped finely
2⅓ cups (600ml) bottled tomato sauce
2 teaspoons balsamic vinegar
13oz penne pasta
¼ cup (1oz) finely grated Parmesan cheese

1 Heat oil in large saucepan; cook onion, garlic and chili, stirring, until onion softens. Add sauce and vinegar; bring to the boil. Reduce heat; simmer, uncovered, about 5 minutes or until sauce thickens slightly.
2 Meanwhile, cook pasta in large saucepan of boiling water until tender; drain. Combine pasta with sauce; sprinkle with cheese.

prep & cook time 25 minutes **serves** 4
nutritional count per serving 8.6g total fat (2.1g saturated fat); 498 cal; 84.2g carbohydrate; 16.1g protein; 7.8g fiber

baked penne with sweet potato and spinach

2 medium red onions (12oz), cut into wedges

2 small sweet potatoes (1lb 5oz), sliced thickly

2 tablespoons olive oil

13oz penne pasta

9oz frozen spinach, thawed, drained

1½ cups (13oz) ricotta cheese

1 clove garlic, crushed

¼ cup (60ml) cream

2 x 14oz cans crushed tomatoes

¼ cup (1oz) pine nuts

½ cup (1oz) finely grated Parmesan cheese

1 Preheat oven to 425°F.

2 Combine onion and sweet potato with oil in large baking dish; roast, uncovered, stirring once, about 40 minutes or until tender.

3 Cook pasta in large saucepan of boiling water until tender; drain.

4 Combine pasta in large bowl with spinach, ricotta, garlic, cream and tomatoes.

5 Spread sweet potato mixture over base of 12-cup baking dish. Top with pasta mixture; sprinkle with nuts and Parmesan. Bake, covered, in oven, 10 minutes. Uncover; bake about 5 minutes or until browned lightly.

prep & cook time 1 hour 10 minutes **serves** 6
nutritional count per serving 25.3g total fat (9.8g saturated fat); 586 cal; 63.4g carbohydrate; 21.9g protein; 8.4g fiber

ravioli & tortellini

Ravioli are little pillows of pasta stuffed with a variety of delicious fillings including meat, fish, cheese and vegetables. Tortellini are very similar, but are formed into a ring shape.

seafood ravioli with sesame dressing

9oz uncooked medium jumbo shrimp,
   shelled, chopped coarsely
4oz red fish fillets, chopped coarsely
2 cloves garlic, crushed
1in piece fresh ginger, grated
½ teaspoon sesame oil
24 wonton wrappers
12 scallops (11oz)
1 egg white, beaten lightly
½ cup loosely packed coriander leaves
2 green onions, sliced thinly
sesame dressing
2 tablespoons kecap manis
2 tablespoons rice wine vinegar
¼ teaspoon sesame oil
1 fresh long red chili, sliced thinly

1 Blend or process shrimp, fish, garlic, ginger and sesame oil until mixture forms a coarse paste. Place one heaped teaspoon of shrimp mixture in center of each of 12 wrappers; top each with a scallop. Brush edges of wrappers with egg white; top each with another wrapper, pressing edges firmly.
2 Using blunt edge of 2in round cutter, gently press down around filling to enclose securely. Using 3in cutter, cut filled ravioli into rounds; discard excess wrapper pastry. Rest ravioli on a tea-towel-lined tray.
3 Make sesame dressing.
4 Cook ravioli, in batches, in large saucepan of boiling water, about 3 minutes or until ravioli float to the surface. Remove ravioli from pan; drain.
5 Divide ravioli among serving plates; drizzle with dressing, sprinkle with coriander and onion.
sesame dressing Combine ingredients in screw-top jar; shake well.

prep & cook time 40 minutes **serves** 4
nutritional count per serving 2.8g total fat (0.6g saturated fat); 147 cal; 2.7g carbohydrate; 27.2g protein; 0.6g fiber

chicken ravioli with tarragon sauce

1lb 11oz ground chicken
2 green onions, sliced thinly
2 teaspoons finely grated lemon rind
56 gow gee wrappers
1 egg, beaten lightly
2 teaspoons olive oil
1 medium onion (5oz), chopped finely
2 cloves garlic, crushed
½ cup (125ml) dry white wine
1 tablespoon Dijon mustard
2⅓ cups (580ml) cream
2 tablespoons finely shredded fresh tarragon

1 Combine chicken, green onion and rind in bowl.
2 Brush one wrapper at a time with egg. Place a rounded teaspoon of the chicken mixture in center of wrapper. Fold over to enclose filling; press edge to seal. Repeat to make a total of 56 ravioli. Place ravioli, in single layer, on tray. Cover; refrigerate 30 minutes.
3 Heat oil in medium saucepan; cook brown onion and garlic, stirring, until onion is just browned. Add wine; cook, stirring, about 5 minutes or until wine reduces by half. Stir in mustard and cream; cook sauce, stirring, until mixture just boils.
4 Meanwhile, cook pasta in large saucepan of boiling water until pasta floats to the top; drain. Add pasta and tarragon to cream sauce. Toss gently until pasta is warmed through.

prep & cook time 55 minutes (+ refrigeration) **serves** 8
nutritional count per serving 41.5g total fat (23.5g saturated fat); 507 cal; 4.9g carbohydrate; 26.9g protein; 0.5g fiber

ravioli with pumpkin and sage sauce

1 tablespoon olive oil
8 large fresh sage leaves
1lb 2oz pumpkin, cut into ½in cubes
4 green onions, chopped coarsely
1 tablespoon thinly shredded fresh sage
1lb 11oz ravioli
1 tablespoon balsamic vinegar
¾ cup (180ml) cream
¾ cup (180ml) vegetable stock

1 Heat oil in large frying pan, add sage leaves; cook, stirring gently, until bright green and crisp. Drain on absorbent paper.
2 Cook pumpkin in same pan, uncovered, stirring occasionally, about 15 minutes or until browned lightly and just tender. Add onion and shredded sage; cook, stirring, 1 minute. Remove from pan; cover to keep warm.
3 Meanwhile, cook pasta in large saucepan of boiling water until tender; drain. Cover to keep warm.
4 Place vinegar, cream and stock in same cleaned frying pan; bring to the boil. Reduce heat, simmer, uncovered, 5 minutes. Add pumpkin mixture; cook, stirring, over low heat until sauce is heated through.
5 Serve pasta topped with sauce and fried sage leaves.

prep & cook time 35 minutes **serves** 4
nutritional count per serving 34g total fat (17.7g saturated fat); 521 cal; 34.5g carbohydrate; 17.8g protein; 4.3g fiber

We used a roasted vegetable ravioli, but you can use any variety of ravioli or other filled pasta you like.

scallop mousse ravioli in star anise broth

3oz angel hair pasta

11oz scallops

2 tablespoons coarsely chopped fresh coriander

2 teaspoons finely chopped fresh lemon grass

½in piece fresh ginger, grated

2 tablespoons fish sauce

2 egg whites

1 litre (4 cups) chicken stock

1½ cups (375ml) fish stock

2 star anise

40 wonton wrappers

1 green onion

1 tablespoon drained sliced pink pickled ginger

1 fresh small red thai chili, sliced finely

⅓ cup firmly packed coriander leaves

1 Cook pasta in medium saucepan of boiling water until tender; drain. Using kitchen scissors, chop into random lengths; reserve.

2 Blend or process scallops, chopped coriander, lemon grass, fresh ginger, sauce and egg whites until mixture forms a smooth paste.

3 Bring stocks and star anise to the boil in large saucepan. Reduce heat; simmer, covered, while making ravioli.

4 Place level tablespoons of scallop mixture in the center of 20 wonton wrappers; brush edges lightly with a little water. Top each with remaining wonton wrappers; press edges together to seal ravioli.

5 Trim onion; cut crossways into quarters, cut each quarter lengthways into thin strips. Cut pickled ginger into thin strips. Divide onion, pickled ginger, noodles, chili and coriander leaves among soup bowls.

6 Cook ravioli, in batches, in large saucepan of boiling water until ravioli floats to the top; drain. Divide among bowls. Discard star anise from hot broth; ladle over ravioli.

prep & cook time 1 hour **serves** 4
nutritional count per serving 3g total fat
(1g saturated fat); 215 cal; 19.6g carbohydrate;
26.4g protein; 1.1g fiber

ravioli with fennel & leek

3oz butter

2 tablespoons olive oil

1 large fennel bulb (1lb 4oz), trimmed, sliced thinly

1 large leek (1lb 2oz), chopped finely

⅓ cup (80ml) dry white wine

1 tablespoon white sugar

11oz ground beef

10oz packet wonton wrappers

1 egg, beaten lightly

2 tablespoons lemon juice

1 clove garlic, crushed

1 tablespoon finely chopped fresh chives

1 Heat a quarter of the butter with half of the oil in large frying pan; cook fennel and leek, stirring, 5 minutes. Stir in wine and sugar; bring to the boil. Reduce heat; simmer, covered, stirring occasionally, about 20 minutes or until liquid is absorbed and vegetables are caramelized.

2 Meanwhile, combine mince with remaining oil in medium bowl.

3 Place a heaped teaspoon of mince mixture in center of one wonton wrapper, brush edges with a little egg; top with another wrapper, press edges together to seal. Repeat with remaining mince mixture, wrappers and egg.

4 Cook pasta, in batches, in large saucepan of boiling water until pasta floats to the top and mince is cooked through; drain. Toss pasta in large bowl with remaining chopped butter, juice and garlic.

5 Divide pasta among serving bowls; top with caramelized fennel and leek, sprinkle with chives.

prep & cook time 55 minutes **serves** 4
nutritional count per serving 33.2g total fat (14.9g saturated fat); 469 cal; 11.5g carbohydrate; 26.7g protein; 4.2g fiber

cheese & spinach tortellini with gorgonzola sauce

1oz butter
2 tablespoons all-purpose flour
1 cup (250ml) milk
¾ cup (180ml) cream
4oz gorgonzola cheese, chopped coarsely
1lb 11oz packaged cheese and spinach tortellini
¼ cup loosely packed fresh flat-leaf parsley leaves

1 Melt butter in medium saucepan, add flour; cook, stirring, about 2 minutes or until mixture bubbles and thickens. Gradually stir in milk and cream; bring to the boil. Reduce heat; simmer, uncovered, until sauce boils and thickens. Remove from heat; stir in cheese.
2 Meanwhile, cook pasta in large saucepan of boiling water until pasta floats to the top; drain.
3 Combine pasta with sauce; sprinkle with parsley.

prep & cook time 20 minutes **serves** 4
nutritional count per serving 58.5g total fat (37.4g saturated fat); 895 cal; 56.2g carbohydrate; 34g protein; 5.8g fiber

Ravioli or gnocchi can be substituted for the tortellini. It's best to choose a ricotta-and-spinach-filled tortellini (or even just a plain ricotta-filled version) when making this sauce, as it doesn't marry overly well with meat-filled pastas.

ricotta & pepper ravioli with rocket dressing

3 large red peppers (2lb 4oz)
2 green onions, chopped finely
1 clove garlic, crushed
2½ cups (1lb 5oz) ricotta cheese
72 wonton wrappers
11oz baby rocket leaves
½ cup (125ml) olive oil
2 tablespoons lemon juice
2 tablespoons balsamic vinegar
2 teaspoons white sugar
1 clove garlic, quartered, extra
¼ cup (1oz) shaved Parmesan cheese

1 Quarter peppers; discard seeds and membranes. Roast, skin-side up, under very hot grill until skin blisters and blackens. Cover pepper in plastic or paper for 5 minutes; peel away skin then chop pepper finely.
2 Combine pepper, onion, garlic and ricotta in bowl.
3 Place level tablespoons of the pepper filling in the center of 36 wonton wrappers; brush edges lightly with a little water. Top each with remaining wonton wrappers; press edges together to seal.
4 Reserve approximately a fifth of the rocket. Process remaining rocket, oil, juice, vinegar, sugar and extra garlic until pureed. Strain into medium jug; discard pulp.
5 Cook pasta in large saucepan of boiling water until pasta floats to the top; drain. Serve pasta drizzled with rocket dressing; top with cheese and reserved rocket.

prep & cook time 1 hour 10 minutes **serves** 6
nutritional count per serving 33.1g total fat (10.9g saturated fat); 452 cal; 12.2g carbohydrate; 25.9g protein; 2.6g fiber

ravioli with asian greens

1 tablespoon sesame oil
4 green onions, chopped finely
1½in piece fresh ginger (1oz), grated
4 cloves garlic, crushed
1lb ground chicken
2 tablespoons soy sauce
½ teaspoon five-spice powder
4oz Napa cabbage, sliced thinly
¼ cup coarsely chopped fresh coriander
40 wonton wrappers
1½ cups (375ml) chicken stock
1½ cups (375ml) water
2 fresh small red thai chilies, chopped finely
2 tablespoons soy sauce, extra
1 tablespoon char siu sauce
¼ cup (60ml) chinese cooking wine
1lb 2oz baby bok choy, quartered lengthways
5oz snow peas, trimmed, halved

1 Heat oil in wok; stir-fry onion, ginger and garlic until onion softens. Add ground chicken; stir-fry until meat changes color. Add soy sauce, five-spice and Napa cabbage; stir-fry until Napa cabbage is tender. Stir in coriander; cool 10 minutes.
2 Place 1 level tablespoon of the mixture in center of one wrapper; brush around edges with water. Top with another wrapper; press edges together to seal. Repeat with remaining mince mixture and wrappers.
3 Add stock, the water, chili, extra soy sauce, char siu sauce and cooking wine to same cleaned wok; bring to the boil. Add pasta to wok; boil until pasta floats to the top. Using slotted spoon, remove pasta from stock mixture; cover to keep warm.
4 Cook bok choy and snow peas in stock mixture until vegetables are tender.
5 Divide pasta and vegetables among serving bowls; ladle over stock mixture.

prep & cook time 1 hour 10 minutes **serves** 4
nutritional count per serving 15.8g total fat (3.8g saturated fat); 517 cal; 52.9g carbohydrate; 35.9g protein; 4.3g fiber

ravioli with spinach and sage

1lb 2oz ricotta and spinach ravioli
1¼ cups (300ml) cream
¼ cup (1oz) finely grated Parmesan cheese
4oz baby spinach leaves
1 tablespoon small sage leaves
2 tablespoons roasted pine nuts
2 tablespoons Parmesan cheese flakes

1 Cook pasta in large saucepan of boiling water until tender; drain.
2 Meanwhile, place cream and grated cheese in small saucepan; bring to the boil. Reduce heat, simmer, uncovered, 5 minutes or until mixture thickens slightly.
3 Add cream mixture, spinach and sage to ravioli; toss gently to combine.
4 Divide among serving plates, top with pine nuts and cheese flakes.

prep & cook time 25 minutes **serves** 4
nutritional count per serving 49g total fat (28.8g saturated fat); 592 cal; 21.4g carbohydrate; 16.1g protein; 3.2g fiber

ravioli with tomato, pea and basil sauce

2 teaspoons olive oil
6 slices pancetta (3oz)
1 clove garlic, crushed
25oz bottled tomato sauce
¼ cup (60ml) dry white wine
2 tablespoons finely chopped fresh basil
1 cup 4oz frozen peas
1lb 6oz spinach and ricotta ravioli

1 Heat oil in large frying pan; cook pancetta until crisp. Drain on absorbent paper; break into pieces.
2 Cook garlic in same pan, stirring, 1 minute. Add sauce, wine and basil; bring to the boil. Add peas, reduce heat; simmer, uncovered, 15 minutes.
3 Meanwhile, cook ravioli in large saucepan of boiling water, uncovered, until just tender; drain. Return ravioli to pan, add sauce; toss to combine. Divide among serving bowls; top with pancetta.

prep & cook time 25 minutes **serves** 4
nutritional count per serving 12.8g total fat (4.1g saturated fat); 381 cal; 46.6g carbohydrate; 20.1g protein; 7.4g fiber

rigatoni

Rigatoni, a ridged, tube-shaped pasta, is ideal for 'pasta al forno' (baked dishes) because it is wide and the hearty fillings cling to the indentations around the edges.

rigatoni with eggplant sauce

¼ cup (60ml) olive oil
1 medium onion (5oz), chopped finely
2 stalks celery (11oz), trimmed, chopped finely
1 clove garlic, crushed
2 tablespoons brandy (optional)
1 medium eggplant (11oz), sliced thinly
2⅓ cups (21oz) bottled tomato sauce
½ cup (5oz) tomato paste
½ cup (125ml) water
13oz rigatoni pasta
¼ cup (1oz) finely grated Parmesan cheese

1 Heat oil in large saucepan; cook onion, celery and garlic, stirring, until onion softens. Add brandy; cook, stirring, until brandy evaporates. Add eggplant; cook, stirring, until tender.
2 Add sauce, paste and the water to pan; bring to the boil. Reduce heat; simmer, uncovered, about 10 minutes or until sauce thickens slightly.
3 Meanwhile, cook pasta in large saucepan of boiling water until tender; drain.
4 Place pasta in large bowl with half the eggplant sauce; toss gently. Divide pasta among serving plates, top with remaining sauce; sprinkle over cheese.

prep & cook time 30 minutes **serves** 4
nutritional count per serving 17g total fat
(3.1g saturated fat); 702 cal; 109g carbohydrate;
16g protein; 10.6g fiber

pancetta and radicchio rigatoni

1lb 2oz rigatoni pasta
6 slices pancetta (3oz)
1oz butter
1 medium leek (13oz), sliced thinly
1 cup (250ml) cream
2 medium radicchio (14oz), trimmed, sliced thinly
½ cup loosely packed fresh flat-leaf parsley leaves
2 teaspoons finely grated lemon rind
⅓ cup (80ml) lemon juice

1 Cook pasta in large saucepan of boiling water, uncovered, until tender; drain.
2 Meanwhile, cook pancetta in heated oiled large frying pan until crisp. Drain on absorbent paper; chop coarsely.
3 Melt butter in same frying pan; cook leek, stirring, until soft. Add cream; bring to the boil. Reduce heat; simmer, uncovered, 2 minutes.
4 Add leek mixture to pasta with half the pancetta and remaining ingredients; toss gently then sprinkle with remaining pancetta.

prep & cook time 25 minutes **serves** 4
nutritional count per serving 34.4g total fat
(21.3g saturated fat); 778 cal; 96.9g carbohydrate;
22g protein; 8.2g fiber

rigatoni with brie, walnut & mushroom sauce

1 tablespoon olive oil
1 clove garlic, crushed
7oz button mushrooms, halved
½ cup (125ml) dry white wine
2 tablespoons wholegrain mustard
2½ cups (600ml) cream
13oz rigatoni pasta
7oz brie cheese, chopped coarsely
1 cup (4oz) walnuts, roasted, chopped coarsely
¼ cup coarsely chopped fresh chives

1 Heat oil in large frying pan; cook garlic and mushrooms, stirring, until mushrooms are just tender. Add wine; boil, uncovered, until wine reduces by half.
2 Add mustard and cream to mushroom mixture; cook, stirring, until sauce thickens slightly.
3 Meanwhile, cook pasta in large saucepan of boiling water until tender; drain.
4 Place pasta, cheese, nuts, chives and sauce in large bowl; toss gently.

prep & cook time 25 minutes **serves** 4
nutritional count per serving 69.9g total fat
(32.4g saturated fat); 1067 cal; 72g carbohydrate;
30.6g protein; 6.4g fiber

rigatoni with broccoli & cauliflower

13oz rigatoni pasta
⅓ cup (80ml) extra virgin olive oil
5 cloves garlic, chopped coarsely
1½ cups (4oz) stale breadcrumbs
13oz cauliflower florets
13oz broccoli florets
⅓ cup (80ml) lemon juice
1 cup coarsely chopped fresh flat-leaf parsley
½ cup (1oz) roasted flaked almonds

1 Cook pasta in large saucepan of boiling water until tender; drain.
2 Meanwhile, heat 2 tablespoons of the oil in large frying pan; cook garlic and breadcrumbs, stirring, until browned lightly. Place in large serving bowl.
3 Heat remaining oil in same pan; cook cauliflower and broccoli, in batches, stirring, until almost tender. Add vegetables, pasta, juice, parsley and nuts to large bowl with breadcrumb mixture; toss to combine.

prep & cook time 40 minutes **serves** 4
nutritional count per serving 26.3g total fat
(3.3g saturated fat); 693 cal; 85g carbohydrate;
22.9g protein; 11.6g fiber

rigatoni with feta & red pepper sauce

13oz rigatoni pasta
2 medium tomatoes (11oz), seeded, sliced thinly
1 small red onion (4oz), sliced thinly
¼ cup fresh flat-leaf parsley leaves
3oz low-fat feta cheese, crumbled
red pepper sauce
1 small red pepper (5oz), quartered, seeds removed
1 clove garlic, crushed
1 teaspoon coarsely chopped fresh thyme
1 tablespoon red wine vinegar
1 tablespoon lemon juice
⅓ cup (80ml) vegetable stock

1 Make red pepper sauce.
2 Cook pasta in large saucepan of boiling water until tender; drain. Toss hot pasta with tomato, onion, parsley and pepper sauce in large bowl; sprinkle with cheese.
red pepper sauce Roast pepper, skin-side up, under very hot grill until skin blackens. Cover with plastic wrap for 5 minutes; peel away skin then chop coarsely. Blend with remaining ingredients until smooth. Sieve and discard solids.

prep & cook time 40 minutes **serves** 4
nutritional count per serving 4.6g total fat
(2.3g saturated fat); 402 cal; 68.4g carbohydrate;
18.3g protein; 5g fiber

For a recipe suitable for vegetarians, use a vegetable stock cube instead of the chicken stock cube.

rigatoni with tomato & red wine sauce

1oz butter
1 medium onion (5oz), chopped finely
1 clove garlic, crushed
15oz can crushed tomatoes
¼ cup (60ml) dry red wine
¼ cup (60ml) water
2 teaspoons tomato paste
1 chicken stock cube (*see note, above*)
1 teaspoon cornflour
1 tablespoon water, extra
1 teaspoon white sugar
2 teaspoons finely chopped fresh basil
1 tablespoon finely chopped fresh flat-leaf parsley
13oz rigatoni pasta

1 Melt butter in large frying pan; cook onion and garlic, stirring, over medium heat until onion is soft. Add undrained tomatoes, wine, the water, paste and crumbled stock cube; bring to the boil. Reduce heat; simmer, uncovered, 10 minutes.
2 Stir blended cornflour and the extra water into tomato mixture; stir constantly over high heat until mixture boils and thickens. Stir in sugar and herbs.
3 Meanwhile, cook pasta in large saucepan of boiling water until tender; drain.
4 Serve sauce spooned over pasta.

prep & cook time 30 minutes **serves** 4
nutritional count per serving 7.5g total fat (4.3g saturated fat); 426 cal; 71.4g carbohydrate; 12.2g protein; 5.1g fiber

rigatoni with zucchini, lemon and mint

1lb 2oz rigatoni pasta
¼ cup (60ml) olive oil
2 cloves garlic, crushed
3 medium zucchini (13oz), grated coarsely
¾ cup (6oz) ricotta cheese
1 cup coarsely chopped fresh mint
½ cup (3oz) roasted slivered almonds
2 tablespoons lemon juice

1 Cook pasta in large saucepan of boiling water until tender; drain.
2 Meanwhile, heat oil in large frying pan; cook garlic and zucchini, stirring, 2 minutes. Add cheese; cook, stirring, until just heated through.
3 Combine zucchini mixture and pasta in serving bowl with remaining ingredients.

prep & cook time 20 minutes **serves** 4
nutritional count per serving 30.3g total fat
(6g saturated fat); 744 cal; 88.9g carbohydrate;
23.9g protein; 8.3g fiber

chicken, mushroom & asparagus creamy pasta bake

13oz rigatoni pasta
2oz butter
1lb 5oz chicken breast fillets, cut into ½in pieces
4oz button mushrooms, sliced thinly
2 tablespoons all-purpose flour
2 cups (500ml) milk
½ cup (1oz) coarsely grated pecorino cheese
1¼ cups (5oz) coarsely grated cheddar cheese
6oz asparagus, trimmed, chopped coarsely
¼ cup coarsely chopped fresh flat-leaf parsley

1 Preheat oven to 400°F.
2 Cook pasta in large saucepan of boiling water until tender; drain.
3 Meanwhile, heat a third of the butter in large frying pan; cook chicken, in batches, until browned and cooked through.
4 Heat remaining butter in same pan; cook mushrooms, stirring, until tender. Add flour; cook, stirring, 1 minute. Gradually add milk, stirring over medium heat until mixture boils and thickens. Stir in chicken, ¼ cup of the pecorino, ¾ cup of the cheddar and the asparagus.
5 Combine chicken mixture and drained pasta in 10-cup ovenproof dish; sprinkle with remaining cheeses. Cook, uncovered, in oven about 15 minutes or until top browns lightly. Serve pasta bake sprinkled with parsley.

prep & cook time 50 minutes **serves** 4
nutritional count per serving 37.3g total fat (22.3g saturated fat); 903 cal; 75.2g carbohydrate; 64g protein; 4.8g fiber

rigatoni with spicy pork sausages

11oz thin spicy pork sausages
13oz rigatoni pasta
1 medium onion (5oz), chopped finely
1 clove garlic, crushed
1lb 2oz tomato and basil pasta sauce
½ cup (3oz) seeded black olives
4oz baby rocket leaves
⅓ cup (1oz) grated Parmesan cheese

1 Cook sausages in large frying pan until browned all over and cooked through. Drain on absorbent paper; slice thickly.
2 Meanwhile, cook pasta in large saucepan of boiling water until tender; drain. Reserve ½ cup of the cooking liquid.
3 Cook onion and garlic in same frying pan until soft. Add pasta sauce, sausages and olives; simmer, uncovered, stirring, until hot.
4 Combine pasta, sauce and reserved cooking liquid in pan; add rocket, toss gently. Serve topped with cheese.

prep & cook time 30 minutes **serves** 4
nutritional count per serving 21g total fat (8.4g saturated fat); 646 cal; 85g carbohydrate; 25g protein; 7.5g fiber

salmon & pea pasta bake

13oz rigatoni pasta
1oz butter
2 tablespoons plain flour
2 cups (500ml) milk
1½ cups (6oz) frozen peas
½ cup (1oz) coarsely grated Parmesan cheese
1¼ cups (5oz) coarsely grated cheddar cheese
15oz can pink salmon, drained

1 Preheat oven to 400°F.
2 Cook pasta in large saucepan of boiling water until tender; drain.
3 Meanwhile, melt butter in medium saucepan, add flour; cook, stirring, until mixture thickens and bubbles. Gradually add milk, stirring until sauce boils and thickens. Stir in peas, ¼ cup Parmesan and ¾ cup cheddar cheese.
4 Combine sauce mixture with pasta and salmon in shallow 10-cup oiled ovenproof dish; sprinkle with remaining combined cheeses. Bake, uncovered, in oven, about 20 minutes or until browned lightly.

prep & cook time 50 minutes **serves** 6
nutritional count per serving 23.8g total fat (13.7g saturated fat); 561 cal; 51.2g carbohydrate; 33.1g protein; 3.9g fiber

risoni

Risoni, a small, rice-shaped pasta very similar to orzo, is often used as an ingredient in soups and salads rather than served on its own.

seafood risoni paella

12 uncooked medium jumbo shrimp (1lb 3oz)
9oz small mussels
11oz firm white fish fillets
2 tablespoons olive oil
1 small onion (3oz), chopped finely
4 cloves garlic, crushed
1lb 2oz risoni pasta
pinch saffron threads
1 cup (250ml) dry white wine
6 small tomatoes (1lb 3oz), seeded, chopped coarsely
2 tablespoons tomato paste
1 teaspoon finely grated orange rind
4 sprigs fresh marjoram
1 liter (4 cups) vegetable stock, warmed
1½ cups (6oz) frozen peas
5oz calamari rings

1 Shell and devein shrimp, leaving tails intact. Scrub mussels; remove beards. Cut fish into 1in pieces.
2 Heat oil in large deep frying pan; cook onion and garlic, stirring, until onion softens. Add pasta and saffron; stir to coat in onion mixture. Stir in wine, tomato, paste, rind and marjoram; cook, stirring, until wine has almost evaporated.
3 Add 1 cup of the stock; stir until liquid is absorbed. Add remaining stock; cook, stirring, until pasta is almost tender.
4 Place peas and all the seafood in pan on top of risoni mixture; do not stir to combine. Cover pan, reduce heat; simmer about 10 minutes or until seafood has changed in color and mussels have opened (discard any that do not).

prep & cook time 1 hour **serves** 4
nutritional count per serving 14.6g total fat (2.9g saturated fat); 807 cal; 94.6g carbohydrate; 58.1g protein; 9g fiber

This recipe can be made in a traditional paella pan if you own one, otherwise a deep frying pan or wok with a tight-fitting lid will suffice. Serve the paella straight from the pan at the table.

pea & ham soup with risoni

2 teaspoons olive oil
1 medium onion (5oz), chopped coarsely
2 teaspoons ground cumin
10 cups water
2 stalks celery (11oz), trimmed, chopped coarsely
2 dried bay leaves
3lb 6oz ham bone
1 cup (8oz) risoni pasta
2 cups (9oz) frozen peas
2 tablespoons finely chopped fresh mint

1 Heat oil in large saucepan; cook onion, stirring, until softened. Add cumin; cook, stirring, until fragrant. Add the water, celery, bay leaves and ham bone; bring to the boil. Simmer, covered, 1 hour, skimming occasionally.
2 Remove bone; when cool enough to handle, cut ham from bone; discard skin, fat and bone. Shred ham finely.
3 Return soup to the boil; stir in ham, pasta and peas. Cook, uncovered, about 5 minutes or until pasta is tender. Sprinkle bowls of soup with mint.

prep & cook time 1 hour 30 minutes **serves** 6
nutritional count per serving 3g total fat
(0.6g saturated fat); 194 cal; 30g carbohydrate;
9g protein; 4.6g fiber

To make this a meal suitable for vegetarians, substitute vegetable stock for the chicken stock.

risoni with spinach & semi-dried tomatoes

1oz butter
2 medium onions (11oz), chopped finely
3 cloves garlic, crushed
1lb 2oz risoni pasta
4 cups (1 liter) chicken stock (*see note, above*)
½ cup (125ml) dry white wine
5oz semi-dried tomatoes, halved
4oz baby spinach leaves
⅓ cup (1oz) finely grated Parmesan cheese

1 Melt butter in large saucepan; cook onion and garlic, stirring, until onion softens. Add pasta; stir to coat in butter mixture. Stir in stock and wine; bring to the boil.
2 Reduce heat; simmer over medium heat, stirring, until liquid is absorbed and pasta is just tender. Gently stir in tomato, spinach and cheese.

prep & cook time 30 minutes **serves** 4
nutritional count per serving 12.4g total fat
(6.3g saturated fat); 677 cal; 104.7g carbohydrate;
24.8g protein; 11.2g fiber

mussels & beans à la grecque

1 cup (8oz) risoni pasta
1lb 2oz frozen broad beans
½ cup (125ml) water
½ cup (125ml) dry white wine
2lb 4oz medium mussels, scrubbed
7oz green beans, trimmed, cut into 1in lengths
1 cup (4oz) seeded black olives
1 large red pepper (13oz), chopped coarsely
oregano and red wine vinaigrette
2 teaspoons finely chopped fresh oregano
2 tablespoons red wine vinegar
2 cloves garlic, crushed
1 small onion (3oz), grated finely
½ teaspoon ground cumin
⅓ cup (80ml) extra virgin olive oil

1 Cook pasta and broad beans, separately, in large saucepans of boiling water until tender; drain. Cool beans 10 minutes then peel away gray outer shells.
2 Meanwhile, heat the water and wine in large saucepan. Add mussels; cook, covered, about 10 minutes or until open (discard any that do not). Reserve 16 mussels; cover to keep warm. Remove remaining mussels from shells.
3 Make oregano and red wine vinaigrette.
4 Boil, steam or microwave green beans until just tender; drain. Rinse under cold water; drain.
5 Combine pasta, beans and shelled mussels in large bowl with olives, pepper and vinaigrette; toss gently. Divide among bowls; top with mussels in shells.
oregano and red wine vinaigrette Combine ingredients in screw-top jar; shake well.

prep & cook time 45 minutes **serves** 4
nutritional count per serving 20.6g total fat (3.1g saturated fat); 512 cal; 53.3g carbohydrate; 19.3g protein; 7.5g fiber

risoni with mushrooms, zucchini and green onions

1lb 2oz risoni pasta
1 tablespoon olive oil
2oz butter
3 large zucchini (1lb), sliced thinly
11oz button mushrooms, sliced thinly
2 cloves garlic, crushed
1 tablespoon coarsely chopped fresh oregano
1 tablespoon lemon juice
1 tablespoon red wine vinegar
7oz green onions, sliced thinly
½ cup (1oz) coarsely grated Parmesan cheese

1 Cook pasta in large saucepan of boiling water until tender; drain.
2 Meanwhile, heat oil with half the butter in large frying pan; cook zucchini, stirring, until tender.
3 Add remaining butter to pan with mushrooms, garlic and oregano; cook, stirring, 2 minutes then stir in juice and vinegar. Remove from heat; stir in onion and cheese.
4 Place pasta and zucchini mixture in large serving bowl; toss gently.

prep & cook time 30 minutes **serves** 4
nutritional count per serving 22.2g total fat (11.1g saturated fat); 674 cal; 90.2g carbohydrate; 23.1g protein; 9.4g fiber

grilled lamb and risoni with mustard sauce

1lb lamb fillets
1lb 2oz risoni pasta
1 tablespoon olive oil
2 cloves garlic, crushed
1¼ cups (300ml) cream
¼ cup (3oz) wholegrain mustard
1 cup (4oz) frozen peas

1 Cook lamb, in batches, on heated oiled grill plate (or grill or barbecue) until browned and cooked as desired. Cover; stand 5 minutes then slice thickly.
2 Meanwhile, cook pasta in large saucepan of boiling water until tender; drain.
3 Heat oil in small saucepan; cook garlic, stirring, until fragrant. Add cream and mustard; bring to the boil. Reduce heat, simmer, uncovered, 2 minutes. Add peas; bring to the boil, then remove from heat.
4 Place lamb, pasta and sauce in large bowl; toss gently.

prep & cook time 35 minutes **serves** 4
nutritional count per serving 43.1g total fat (24.2g saturated fat); 936 cal; 90.4g carbohydrate; 43g protein; 6.9g fiber

chicken and fresh pea risoni

14oz chicken breast fillets
4 cups chicken stock
11oz sugar snap peas, trimmed
1 cup (6oz) frozen peas
1 tablespoon olive oil
1 small leek (7oz), sliced thinly
1 clove garlic, crushed
1lb 2oz risoni pasta
½ cup (125ml) dry white wine
1 tablespoon white wine vinegar
1 tablespoon finely chopped fresh tarragon

1 Place chicken and stock in medium frying pan; bring to the boil. Reduce heat, simmer, uncovered, 10 minutes or until cooked through. Remove chicken from pan; reserve stock. Slice chicken thinly.
2 Boil, steam or microwave peas, separately, until just tender; drain.
3 Heat oil in large saucepan; cook leek and garlic, stirring, until leek softens. Add risoni; stir to coat in leek mixture. Add wine; stir until wine is almost absorbed. Add reserved stock; bring to the boil. Reduce heat, simmer, uncovered, stirring occasionally, until stock is absorbed and risoni is just tender. Stir in vinegar; remove from heat. Gently stir in chicken, peas and tarragon.

prep & cook time 35 minutes **serves** 4
nutritional count per serving 9.6g total fat (2g saturated fat); 670 cal; 97.1g carbohydrate; 42.5g protein; 7.6g fiber

braised veal rolls with pasta & olives

4 large red peppers (3lb 2oz)
9oz spinach leaves
8 veal steaks (1lb 7oz)
¼ cup (60ml) olive oil
2 medium onions (11oz), chopped finely
2 cloves garlic, crushed
15oz can tomato puree
⅓ cup (80ml) dry red wine
2 teaspoons brown sugar
1 cup (8oz) risoni pasta
¾ cup (3oz) seeded black olives
¼ cup fresh basil leaves

1 Quarter peppers; discard seeds and membranes. Roast under hot grill, skin-side up, until skin blisters and blackens. Cover pepper pieces in plastic or paper for 5 minutes then peel away skin.
2 Place spinach leaves over veal steaks; top with two pepper pieces. Roll veal tightly; secure with toothpicks.
3 Heat 2 tablespoons of the oil in large saucepan. Cook veal, in batches, until browned all over; drain on absorbent paper. Heat remaining oil in pan; cook onion and garlic, stirring, until onion is soft.
4 Return veal to pan with puree, wine and sugar; simmer, covered, 15 minutes. Add pasta and olives; simmer, covered, about 7 minutes or until pasta is tender.
5 Slice veal; serve with sauce, sprinkle with basil.

prep & cook time 1 hour 35 minutes **serves** 8
nutritional count per serving 8.9g total fat
(1.3g saturated fat); 333 cal; 33g carbohydrate;
25.4g protein; 5.2g fiber

spaghetti

The king of pastas, spaghetti, appears on menus worldwide. Versatile and easy to cook, it seems every region of Italy has created its own sauce to accompany this favourite.

prosciutto-wrapped chicken with spaghetti

8 chicken thigh fillets (1lb 13oz)
¼ cup (1oz) grated Parmesan cheese
1 tablespoon coarsely chopped fresh oregano
7oz mozzarella cheese, coarsely chopped
8 slices prosciutto (4oz)
2 tablespoons olive oil
1 clove garlic, crushed
6 medium tomatoes (2lb), chopped coarsely
1 small brown onion (3oz), chopped finely
¼ cup (60ml) chicken stock
2 teaspoons balsamic vinegar
13oz spaghetti
1 tablespoon coarsely chopped fresh flat-leaf parsley

1 Lightly pound chicken fillets using meat mallet. Sprinkle fillets with combined Parmesan and oregano; top with mozzarella, roll tightly. Wrap prosciutto firmly around open ends to secure cheese; secure roll with toothpicks.
2 Heat half the oil in large saucepan; cook chicken, in batches, until browned all over.
3 Heat remaining oil in pan; cook garlic, tomato and onion, stirring, about 5 minutes or until onion is soft.
4 Return chicken to pan. Add stock and vinegar; simmer, covered, 10 minutes. Turn chicken; simmer, uncovered, about 10 minutes or until chicken is tender. Stir in parsley; remove and discard toothpicks.
5 Meanwhile, cook pasta in large saucepan of boiling water until tender; drain.
6 Place pasta in serving bowl; top with chicken.

prep & cook time 1 hour 15 minutes **serves** 4
nutritional count per serving 39.2g total fat (14.6g saturated fat); 928 cal; 69.7g carbohydrate; 70.8g protein; 6.2g fiber

spaghetti marinara

1 tablespoon olive oil
1 medium onion (5oz), chopped finely
⅓ cup (80ml) dry white wine
⅓ cup (3oz) tomato paste
1lb 14oz can crushed tomatoes
1lb 11oz seafood marinara mix
¼ cup coarsely chopped fresh flat-leaf parsley
13oz spaghetti

1   Heat oil in large frying pan; cook onion until soft.
2   Add wine, paste and undrained tomatoes to pan; bring to the boil. Reduce heat; simmer, uncovered, 10 minutes or until sauce thickens slightly.
3   Add marinara mix to tomato mixture; cook, stirring occasionally, about 5 minutes or until seafood is cooked through. Stir in parsley.
4   Meanwhile, cook pasta in large saucepan of boiling water until tender; drain. Serve marinara over pasta.

prep & cook time 20 minutes **serves** 4
nutritional count per serving 11.6g total fat
(2.3g saturated fat); 681 cal; 76.4g carbohydrate;
59.7g protein; 7.3g fiber

spaghetti with oil and garlic

1lb 2oz spaghetti
⅓ cup (80ml) olive oil
3 cloves garlic, crushed
2 tablespoons finely chopped fresh flat-leaf parsley

1   Cook pasta in large saucepan of boiling water until tender; drain.
2   Meanwhile, heat oil in large frying pan; cook garlic, gently, until golden brown, stir in parsley. Combine garlic mixture with pasta.

prep & cook time 15 minutes **serves** 4
nutritional count per serving 19.6g total fat
(2.8g saturated fat); 587 cal; 85.5g carbohydrate;
14.2g protein; 4.6g fiber

spaghetti puttanesca

¼ cup (60ml) olive oil
2 cloves garlic, crushed
4 medium tomatoes (1lb 5oz), chopped coarsely
½ cup finely chopped fresh flat-leaf parsley
12 stuffed olives, sliced thinly
2oz can anchovy fillets, drained, chopped finely
1 tablespoon finely chopped fresh basil
pinch chili powder
13oz spaghetti

1 Heat oil in medium saucepan; cook garlic until just changed in color.
2 Add tomato, parsley, olives, anchovy, basil and chili powder; cook, stirring, 3 minutes.
3 Meanwhile, cook pasta in large saucepan of boiling water until tender; drain.
4 Combine pasta in large bowl with sauce; toss gently.

prep & cook time 35 minutes **serves** 4
nutritional count per serving 16.5g total fat
(2.4g saturated fat); 494 cal; 67.2g carbohydrate;
15.4g protein; 6.5g fiber

spaghetti with pesto

2 cups coarsely chopped fresh basil
2 tablespoons roasted pine nuts
2 cloves garlic
⅓ cup (80ml) olive oil
¼ cup (1oz) grated Parmesan cheese
13oz spaghetti

1 Blend or process basil, nuts and garlic until smooth. With processor operating, add oil in a thin steady stream; process until mixture is combined. Place pesto in medium bowl; stir in cheese.
2 Cook pasta in large saucepan of boiling water until tender; drain.
3 Combine pasta with pesto in large bowl; toss gently. Serve with flakes of Parmesan cheese, if you like.

prep & cook time 30 minutes **serves** 4
nutritional count per serving 26g total fat
(4.1g saturated fat); 557 cal; 65g carbohydrate;
13.7g protein; 4.3g fiber

If you cook this sauce even longer, until it reduces by half, it makes a good pizza-base sauce or, with capers stirred through it, a delicious topping for chicken or veal scaloppine.

spaghetti napoletana

2 teaspoons olive oil
1 small onion (3oz), chopped finely
3 cloves garlic, crushed
1lb 14oz can crushed tomatoes
¼ cup coarsely chopped, firmly packed fresh basil
⅓ cup coarsely chopped fresh flat-leaf parsley
13oz spaghetti

1 Heat oil in large saucepan; cook onion and garlic, stirring, until onion softens.
2 Add undrained tomatoes; bring to the boil. Reduce heat; simmer, uncovered, about 20 minutes or until reduced by about a third. Stir in basil and parsley.
3 Meanwhile, cook pasta in large saucepan of boiling water until tender; drain. Serve pasta topped with sauce.

prep & cook time 30 minutes **serves** 4
nutritional count per serving 3.8g total fat
(0.5g saturated fat); 390 cal; 71.9g carbohydrate;
12.8g protein; 6.6g fiber

spaghetti with mussels & clams

1lb 2oz mussels
1lb 2oz clams
¼ cup (60ml) dry white wine
¼ cup (60ml) water
1lb 2oz spaghetti
⅓ cup (80ml) extra virgin olive oil
2 cloves garlic, crushed
1 fresh small red thai chili, chopped finely
2 medium tomatoes (11oz), seeded, chopped coarsely
½ cup coarsely chopped fresh flat-leaf parsley

1   Scrub mussels. Rinse clams.
2   Combine wine and the water in large saucepan; bring to the boil. Add mussels and clams; reduce heat. Simmer, covered, until shells open (discard any that do not). Remove seafood from liquid; cover to keep warm. Strain cooking liquid through fine sieve into medium heatproof jug; reserve ⅓ cup of the liquid.
3   Cook pasta in large saucepan of boiling water until tender; drain. Return to pan.
4   Meanwhile, heat oil in large frying pan; cook garlic and chili, stirring, until fragrant. Add tomatoes and reserved cooking liquid; simmer, uncovered, until hot.
5   Add seafood, tomato mixture and parsley to pasta; toss gently to combine.

prep & cook time 35 minutes **serves** 6
nutritional count per serving 13.5g total fat (2g saturated fat); 435 cal; 59.2g carbohydrate; 15g protein; 3.9g fiber

spaghetti with herbed ricotta

1lb 2oz spaghetti
2¼ cups (1lb) ricotta cheese
3 egg yolks
¾ cup (180ml) milk
⅓ cup coarsely chopped fresh flat-leaf parsley
¼ cup coarsely chopped fresh basil
3 green onions, chopped finely
2 cloves garlic, crushed
¼ cup (1oz) finely grated pepato cheese

1 Cook pasta in large saucepan of boiling water until tender; drain.
2 Meanwhile, whisk ricotta, egg yolks and milk in large bowl until smooth; stir in herbs, onion, garlic and pepato.
3 Add pasta to ricotta mixture; toss gently.

prep & cook time 25 minutes **serves** 4
nutritional count per serving 20.2g total fat (10.8g saturated fat); 672 cal; 89.4g carbohydrate; 30g protein; 4.9g fiber

Pepato is an Italian sheep-milk cheese, most often pecorino, studded with peppercorns. It is available from some delicatessens and specialty cheese shops. If you can't find it, use pecorino or Parmesan cheese with a good grinding of black pepper.

spaghetti with rocket and pine nuts

1lb 2oz spaghetti
⅓ cup (80ml) olive oil
2 cloves garlic, crushed
2 fresh small red thai chilies, chopped finely
½ cup (3oz) roasted pine nuts
1 cup (3oz) Parmesan cheese flakes
7oz baby rocket leaves

1 Cook pasta in large saucepan of boiling water until tender; drain.
2 Heat oil in small saucepan; cook garlic and chili, stirring, about 30 seconds or until garlic just softens and is fragrant (do not brown).
3 Place hot pasta and garlic mixture in large bowl with nuts, cheese and rocket; toss gently.

prep & cook time 20 minutes **serves** 4
nutritional count per serving 40.5g total fat (7.8g saturated fat); 828 cal; 87.5g carbohydrate; 25.6g protein; 6.2g fiber

spaghetti & meatballs

2 tablespoons olive oil
2 cloves garlic, crushed
1 medium onion (5oz), sliced thinly
½ cup (125ml) dry red wine
2 cups bottled tomato sauce
½ cup (125ml) chicken stock
¼ cup coarsely chopped fresh basil
13oz spaghetti
⅓ cup (1oz) grated Parmesan cheese
meatballs
2lb 4oz ground beef
1 small green pepper (5oz), chopped finely
1 small onion (3oz), chopped finely
2 cloves garlic, crushed
¼ cup coarsely chopped fresh flat-leaf parsley
1 egg
1 cup (3oz) stale breadcrumbs
1 teaspoon finely grated lemon rind
½ cup (5oz) sun-dried tomato pesto

1 Make meatballs.
2 Heat oil in large frying pan; cook meatballs, in batches, until browned all over. Drain on absorbent paper.
3 Cook garlic and onion in same pan, stirring, until onion softens. Add wine; bring to the boil. Reduce heat; simmer, uncovered, about 5 minutes or until mixture is reduced by half. Add sauce and stock; bring to the boil.
4 Return meatballs to pan, reduce heat; simmer, uncovered, about 10 minutes or until meatballs are cooked through. Stir in basil.
5 Meanwhile, cook pasta in large saucepan of boiling water until tender; drain.
6 Divide pasta among serving bowls; top with meatballs and sauce, sprinkle with cheese.
meatballs Combine ingredients in large bowl; roll level tablespoons of mince mixture into balls (*see note, below*).

prep & cook time 40 minutes **serves** 4
nutritional count per serving 50.7g total fat (16.1g saturated fat); 1228 cal; 113g carbohydrate; 70g protein; 9g fiber

We've made twice the number of meatballs required to serve four; freeze half the meatballs for future use by placing the uncooked meatballs in a single layer on a tray, cover; freeze until solid. Remove meatballs from tray and place in either a storage container that has a tight-fitting lid, or a sealable plastic bag; return to freezer. Frozen meatballs can be thawed, then cooked directly in the pasta sauce.

spaghetti with zucchini, tomato and ricotta

1lb 2oz spaghetti
¼ cup (60ml) olive oil
4 medium zucchini (1lb 1oz), cut into 2in lengths
3 cloves garlic, sliced thinly
1lb 2oz cherry tomatoes
4oz baby rocket leaves
1¼ cups (9oz) firm ricotta cheese, crumbled

1 Cook pasta in large saucepan of boiling water until tender; drain.
2 Meanwhile, heat oil in large frying pan; cook zucchini, stirring, until just tender. Add garlic and tomatoes; cook, stirring occasionally, until tomatoes split and soften.
3 Place pasta, zucchini mixture and rocket in large bowl; toss gently. Serve topped with cheese.

prep & cook time 25 minutes **serves** 4
nutritional count per serving 22.8g total fat (6.7g saturated fat); 685 cal; 91.1g carbohydrate; 24g protein; 8.3g fiber

Many varieties of already cooked white beans are available canned, among them cannellini, butter and haricot beans; any of these are suitable for this recipe.

spaghetti with tomato and white beans

⅓ cup (80ml) vegetable stock
1 small red onion (4oz), chopped finely
1 clove garlic, crushed
1 cup (250ml) dry white wine
½ teaspoon white sugar
2 cups (500ml) bottled tomato pasta sauce
1lb 2oz spaghetti
1 tablespoon coarsely chopped fresh oregano
2 tablespoons rinsed, drained capers, chopped coarsely
½ cup (2oz) seeded black olives, quartered
11oz can white beans, rinsed, drained
2 tablespoons coarsely chopped fresh flat-leaf parsley

1 Heat half the stock in medium saucepan, add onion and garlic; cook, stirring, until onion is soft. Stir in wine, remaining stock, sugar and sauce; bring to the boil. Reduce heat, simmer, uncovered, until sauce thickens slightly.
2 Meanwhile, cook pasta in large saucepan of boiling water until tender; drain.
3 Stir remaining ingredients into sauce; cook, stirring, until hot. Serve spaghetti with tomato and white beans.

prep & cook time 30 minutes **serves** 4
nutritional count per serving 2.9g total fat
(0.5g saturated fat); 593 cal; 107.3g carbohydrate;
18.3g protein; 8.8g fiber

spaghetti with anchovies, olives and rocket

13oz spaghetti
14oz grape tomatoes
¼ cup (60ml) olive oil
4 drained anchovy fillets, chopped
2 cloves garlic, crushed
2 fresh long red chilies, sliced thinly
4oz black olives, seeded, halved
4oz baby rocket leaves

1 Cook pasta in large saucepan of boiling water, uncovered, until just tender; drain, return pasta to pan.
2 Meanwhile, halve 7oz of the tomatoes.
3 Heat 1 tablespoon of the oil in medium frying pan; cook anchovies, garlic and chili, stirring, until soft and fragrant. Add all tomatoes to pan; stir until combined.
4 Toss tomato mixture through spaghetti with olives, rocket and remaining oil.

prep & cook time 30 minutes **serves** 4
nutritional count per serving 15.4g total fat (2.2g saturated fat); 489 cal; 71.4g carbohydrate; 12.9g protein; 5.6g fiber

This recipe makes a double quantity of the Bolognese sauce. Freeze any leftover Bolognese sauce for up to three months. The leftover sauce can be used for the *beef, garlic and Swiss chard pasta bake* **on page 92.**

spaghetti bolognese

1 tablespoon olive oil
2 large onions (14oz), chopped finely
4 cloves garlic, crushed
2lb 11oz ground beef
2 large carrots (13oz), grated coarsely
⅓ cup (3oz) tomato paste
3 cups (750ml) beef stock
57oz crushed tomatoes
1 tablespoon mixed dried herbs
1lb 2oz spaghetti
¼ cup (1oz) grated Parmesan cheese

1   Heat oil in large saucepan; cook onion and garlic, stirring, until onion softens.
2   Add mince; cook, stirring, until browned. Add carrot and tomato paste; cook, stirring, 5 minutes. Add stock, undrained tomato and herbs; bring to the boil. Reduce heat; simmer, covered, 45 minutes, stirring occasionally. Uncover; simmer a further 45 minutes or until mixture is thickened slightly.
3   About 10 minutes before sauce is ready, cook pasta in large saucepan of boiling water until tender; drain.
4   Serve half the Bolognese with spaghetti, reserve remaining half for later use (*see note, above*). Serve sprinkled with cheese.

prep & cook time 1 hour 55 minutes **serves** 4
nutritional count per serving 9.9g total fat (3.9g saturated fat); 393 cal; 49.1g carbohydrate; 23.9g protein; 4.6g fiber

spaghetti carbonara with peas

4 egg yolks
¾ cup (2oz) finely grated Parmesan cheese
9oz bacon, chopped finely
2 cloves garlic, sliced thinly
1 cup (4oz) frozen peas
13oz spaghetti

1 Combine egg yolks and cheese in small bowl.
2 Cook bacon over heat in medium frying pan about
5 minutes or until starting to crisp. Add garlic; cook, stirring,
1 minute. Add peas; cook, stirring, until heated through.
3 Meanwhile, cook pasta in large saucepan of boiling
water until tender; drain, reserving ¼ cup cooking liquid.
Return pasta to saucepan.
4 Add bacon mixture, egg mixture and reserved cooking
liquid to pasta; stir over heat about 1 minute.
5 Serve pasta sprinkled with extra Parmesan cheese, if you
like.

prep & cook time 25 minutes **serves** 4
nutritional count per serving 15.3g total fat
(6.3g saturated fat); 558 cal; 66.8g carbohydrate;
35g protein; 5.1g fiber

cauliflower and chili spaghetti

¼ cup (60ml) olive oil
1lb 9oz small cauliflower florets
⅓ cup (2oz) pine nuts, chopped coarsely
2 cloves garlic, crushed
6 drained anchovies, chopped coarsely
½ teaspoon dried chili flakes
1 tablespoon lemon juice
¼ cup coarsely chopped fresh flat-leaf parsley
13oz spaghetti
2 tablespoons olive oil, extra

1 Heat oil in large frying pan; cook cauliflower, stirring, about 10 minutes or until browned lightly and tender.
2 Add nuts; cook, stirring, until browned lightly. Add garlic, anchovies and chili; cook, stirring, until mixture is fragrant. Stir in lemon juice and parsley.
3 Meanwhile, cook pasta in large saucepan of boiling water until tender; drain.
4 Toss cauliflower mixture with spaghetti and extra oil.

prep & cook time 30 minutes **serves** 4
nutritional count per serving 33.2g total fat
(4g saturated fat); 657 cal; 68.5g carbohydrate;
17.7g protein; 7.3g fiber

classic spaghetti bolognese

2 teaspoons olive oil

6 slices pancetta (3oz), chopped finely

1 large white onion (7oz), chopped finely

1 medium carrot (4oz), chopped finely

2 celery stalks (11oz) trimmed, chopped finely

1lb 5oz ground beef

5oz chicken livers, trimmed, chopped finely

1 cup (250ml) milk

2oz butter

1½ cups (375ml) beef stock

1 cup (250ml) dry red wine

15oz can tomato puree

2 tablespoons tomato paste

¼ cup finely chopped fresh flat-leaf parsley

1lb 11oz fresh spaghetti

½ cup (1oz) shaved Parmesan cheese

1 Heat oil in large heavy-based frying pan; cook pancetta, stirring, until crisp. Add onion, carrot and celery; cook, stirring, until vegetables soften.

2 Add beef and liver to pan; cook, stirring, until beef changes color. Stir in milk and butter; cook, stirring occasionally, until liquid reduces to about half.

3 Add stock, wine, puree and paste to pan; simmer, covered, 1 hour. Uncover; simmer 1 hour. Remove from heat; stir in parsley.

4 Meanwhile, cook pasta in large saucepan of boiling water until tender; drain.

5 Serve pasta topped with Bolognese sauce and cheese.

prep + cook time 2 hours 35 minutes **serves** 6
nutritional count per serving 26.6g total fat (13g saturated fat); 599 cal; 41g carbohydrate; 39.2g protein; 5.5g fiber

You can substitute 1lb 2oz dried spaghetti for the fresh spaghetti, if you prefer.

spaghetti with anchovies and garlic breadcrumbs

1lb 2oz spaghetti
12 slices white bread
2oz butter
2 cloves garlic, crushed
2oz drained anchovy fillets, chopped finely
2 teaspoons finely grated lemon rind
2 tablespoons lemon juice
½ cup finely chopped fresh chives
½ cup (125ml) olive oil

1 Cook pasta in large saucepan of boiling water until tender; drain.
2 Meanwhile, remove and discard crusts from bread; blend or process bread into fine crumbs.
3 Melt butter in medium frying pan; cook garlic and breadcrumbs, stirring, until browned.
4 Place pasta and crumb mixture in large bowl with remaining ingredients; toss gently until combined. Serve with lemon wedges, if desired.

prep & cook time 30 minutes **serves** 4
nutritional count per serving 44.9g total fat (12.9g saturated fat); 1011 cal; 123.6g carbohydrate; 24.3g protein; 7g fiber

summer spaghetti with pea pesto and ham

1lb 2oz spaghetti
2 cups (9oz) frozen peas
2 cloves garlic
¼ cup (1oz) roasted pine nuts
½ cup loosely packed fresh basil leaves
⅓ cup loosely packed fresh mint leaves
½ cup (1oz) flaked Parmesan cheese
2 tablespoons olive oil
7oz finely sliced leg ham
⅓ cup (80ml) lemon juice

1   Cook pasta in large saucepan of boiling water until tender; drain.
2   Meanwhile, to make pea pesto, microwave peas on HIGH (100%) about 2 minutes or until tender; drain. Blend or process peas with garlic, nuts, herbs, cheese and oil until mixture forms a thick puree.
3   Combine pea pesto, ham and juice with pasta in large bowl; serve with extra Parmesan, if you like.

prep & cook time 25 minutes **serves** 6
nutritional count per serving 15.3g total fat (3.1g saturated fat); 480 cal; 60.9g carbohydrate; 21.2g protein; 5.9g fiber

spaghetti with capers and anchovies

13oz spaghetti
2 tablespoons olive oil
3 cloves garlic, sliced thinly
¼ cup (2oz) rinsed, drained baby capers
10 anchovy fillets, chopped finely
1 tablespoon finely grated lemon rind
1 tablespoon lemon juice

1 Cook pasta in large saucepan of boiling water until tender; drain.
2 Meanwhile, heat oil in medium frying pan; cook garlic, stirring, until fragrant. Add capers and anchovies; stir gently until hot. Pour garlic mixture over pasta; stir in rind and juice.

prep & cook time 20 minutes **serves** 4
nutritional count per serving 11.1g total fat (1.7g saturated fat); 426 cal; 65.6g carbohydrate; 13.3g protein; 3.8g fiber

spaghetti with spinach and coppa

13oz spaghetti
⅓ cup (80ml) olive oil
1 clove garlic, crushed
¼ medium red pepper (2oz), chopped finely
½ small onion (1oz), chopped finely
1 fresh small red thai chili, sliced thinly
3oz coppa (smoked pork), chopped finely
8 spinach leaves, shredded finely
2 tablespoons grated Parmesan cheese

1 Cook pasta in large saucepan of boiling water until tender; drain.
2 Meanwhile, heat oil in medium frying pan; cook garlic, pepper, onion, chili and coppa, stirring, 2 minutes. Add spinach; cook, stirring constantly, 2 minutes. Add cheese.
3 Combine pasta and sauce.

prep & cook time 35 minutes **serves** 4
nutritional count per serving 23.5g total fat
(4.6g saturated fat); 549 cal; 65.2g carbohydrate;
17g protein; 4g fiber

pasta salads

Once just a useful way of using up leftover pasta, these days versatile pasta salads can star on their own as a main dish, or add pizzazz as a side dish.

chicken and asparagus pasta salad

You will need to purchase a large barbecued chicken weighing about 2lb for this recipe.

1lb 2oz macaroni pasta
9oz asparagus, trimmed, chopped coarsely
3 cups (1lb 1oz) shredded cooked chicken
7oz button mushrooms, sliced
⅓ cup finely chopped fresh chives
mustard mayo dressing
⅓ cup (3oz) light sour cream
½ cup (5oz) mayonnaise
1 tablespoon lemon juice
1 tablespoon wholegrain mustard

1 Cook pasta in large saucepan of boiling water until tender; drain. Rinse under cold water; drain.
2 Meanwhile, boil, steam or microwave asparagus until just tender; drain.
3 Make mustard mayo dressing.
4 Place pasta and asparagus in large bowl with dressing and remaining ingredients; toss gently.
mustard mayo dressing Combine ingredients in small bowl.

prep & cook time 25 minutes **serves** 4
nutritional count per serving 26.7g total fat (6.9g saturated fat); 826 cal; 94.5g carbohydrate; 47.5g protein; 6.5g fiber

This salad should be assembled just before serving.

pasta with the lot

9oz curly lasagne

5oz salami, sliced thickly

7oz Swiss brown mushrooms, sliced thickly

1 medium green pepper (7oz), sliced thinly

2 medium tomatoes (11oz), seeded, sliced thinly

4 drained anchovies, chopped coarsely

4oz kalamata olives, seeded

½ cup (125ml) vegetable or tomato juice

¼ cup (60ml) red wine vinegar

¼ cup (60ml) olive oil

2 cloves garlic, crushed

1   Cook pasta in large saucepan of boiling water until tender; drain. Rinse under cold water; drain.

2   Place pasta in large bowl with salami, mushrooms, pepper, tomato, anchovy, olives and combined remaining ingredients; toss gently.

prep & cook time 25 minutes **serves** 4
nutritional count per serving 29.2g total fat
(6.8g saturated fat); 568 cal; 53.8g carbohydrate;
19.9g protein; 5.3g fiber

We used a hot and spicy Spanish salami in this recipe, but you could use milder cabanossi or pepperoni, if you prefer.

russian penne salad

13oz penne pasta

2 cups (9oz) frozen peas

1lb can whole baby beetroot, drained,
    chopped coarsely

6 green onions, chopped finely

2 cloves garlic, crushed

2 large dill pickles, chopped finely

¼ cup coarsely chopped fresh flat-leaf parsley

1 cup (9oz) sour cream

1 cup (250ml) buttermilk

1   Cook pasta in large saucepan of boiling water until tender; drain. Rinse under cold water; drain.

2   Meanwhile, boil, steam or microwave peas until just tender; drain.

3   Place pasta and peas in large bowl with beetroot, onion, garlic, pickle, parsley and combined sour cream and buttermilk; toss gently.

prep & cook time 25 minutes **serves** 4
nutritional count per serving 26.6g total fat
(16.7g saturated fat); 660 cal; 80.6g carbohydrate;
19.6g protein; 9.6g fiber

greek penne salad

9oz penne pasta

9oz feta cheese

4 medium tomatoes (1lb 5oz), seeded, sliced thinly

½ Lebanese cucumber (5oz), seeded, sliced thinly

1 small red onion (4oz), sliced thinly

¾ cup (4oz) kalamata olives, seeded

¾ cup (4oz) large green olives, seeded

⅓ cup (80ml) olive oil

⅓ cup (80ml) white vinegar

1 teaspoon white sugar

2 tablespoons finely chopped fresh flat-leaf parsley

1 Cook pasta in large saucepan of boiling water until tender; drain. Rinse under cold water; drain.

2 Meanwhile, cut the cheese into baton-shaped pieces about the same size as the pasta.

3 Place pasta and cheese in large bowl with tomato, cucumber, onion, olives and combined remaining ingredients; toss gently.

prep & cook time 30 minutes **serves** 4
nutritional count per serving 34.3g total fat
(12.4g saturated fat); 650 cal; 62.2g carbohydrate;
20.6g protein; 5.4g fiber

Goes well with lemon marinated lamb skewers.

mediterranean pasta salad

13oz elbow macaroni pasta

13oz artichoke hearts in oil

14oz semi-dried tomatoes

¼ cup loosely packed fresh oregano

14oz mozzarella cheese, chopped coarsely

¼ cup (60ml) sherry vinegar

2 cloves garlic, crushed

1 Cook pasta in large saucepan of boiling water until tender; drain. Rinse under cold water; drain.

2 Meanwhile, drain artichokes over small bowl; reserve 2 tablespoons of the oil, discard remaining oil.

3 Quarter artichokes; place in large bowl with pasta, tomatoes, oregano, cheese and combined vinegar, garlic and reserved oil; toss gently.

prep & cook time 25 minutes **serves** 4
nutritional count per serving 31.1g total fat
(15.2g saturated fat); 911 cal; 99g carbohydrate;
48.6g protein; 19.4g fiber

While most of the smoked salmon we buy has been cold-smoked (cured at a low temperature for a fairly long time), hot-smoked salmon (cured at high temperatures for just a few hours) is generally moister and not as salty; it doesn't, however, have the same keeping properties as cold-smoked.

hot-smoked salmon salad

13oz fettuccine pasta
14oz hot-smoked salmon
4oz mizuna
1 medium avocado (9oz), chopped coarsely
1 Lebanese cucumber (5oz), halved, sliced thinly
1 small fennel bulb (7oz), trimmed, sliced thinly
¼ cup (2oz) rinsed, drained baby capers
lemon mustard dressing
1 tablespoon Dijon mustard
2 teaspoons white sugar
2 tablespoons olive oil
1 tablespoon lemon juice

1 Cook pasta in large saucepan of boiling water until tender; drain. Rinse under cold water; drain.
2 Meanwhile, remove any skin and bones from salmon; flake salmon into large pieces. Combine salmon in large bowl with mizuna, avocado, cucumber, fennel and capers.
3 Make dressing.
4 Add pasta and dressing to salmon mixture; toss gently.
lemon mustard dressing Place ingredients in screw-top jar; shake well.

prep & cook time 30 minutes **serves** 4
nutritional count per serving 24.9g total fat (4.5g saturated fat); 656 cal; 69.4g carbohydrate; 35.3g protein; 5.8g fiber

curried pasta salad

1 cup (6oz) small pasta shells
1 medium red pepper (7oz), chopped finely
1 medium green pepper (7oz), chopped finely
2 tablespoons finely chopped fresh chives
5oz button mushrooms, quartered
curry dressing
2 teaspoons curry powder
1 tablespoon superfine sugar
½ cup (125ml) peanut oil
¼ cup (60ml) white vinegar
1 tablespoon cream

1 Cook pasta in large saucepan of boiling water until tender; drain.
2 Meanwhile, make curry dressing.
3 Place pasta in large bowl with peppers, chives and mushrooms. Add dressing; toss to combine.
curry dressing Place curry powder and sugar in small bowl; gradually whisk in oil, vinegar and cream.

prep & cook time 20 minutes **serves** 4
nutritional count per serving 31.3g total fat (6.7g saturated fat); 474 cal; 39.2g carbohydrate; 7.8g protein; 3.3g fiber

Be sure not to overcook the chicken livers or they will be dry and unappealing.

pasta salad with chicken livers & pistachios

9oz curly lasagne
1lb 2oz chicken livers, trimmed
5oz baby rocket leaves
1 tablespoon finely grated lemon rind
⅓ cup (2oz) roasted pistachios
lemon mustard dressing
2 teaspoons Dijon mustard
1 clove garlic, crushed
⅓ cup (80ml) olive oil
¼ cup (60ml) lemon juice

1 Cook pasta in large saucepan of boiling water until tender; drain. Rinse under cold water; drain. Cut pasta lengthways into 1in-thick ribbons.
2 Meanwhile, make lemon mustard dressing.
3 Halve chicken livers; cook, in batches, in heated oiled large frying pan about 2 minutes or until browned and cooked as desired (*see note, above*).
4 Place pasta and liver in large bowl with dressing and remaining ingredients; toss gently.
lemon mustard dressing Combine ingredients in screw-top jar; shake well.

prep & cook time 25 minutes **serves** 4
nutritional count per serving 29.8g total fat (5g saturated fat); 601 cal; 48.5g carbohydrate; 32.9g protein; 3.9g fiber

farfalle with baked salmon, caperberries & dill

2 large red onions (1lb 5oz), cut into wedges
1 cup (6oz) caperberries, rinsed, drained
cooking-oil spray
1 fresh small red thai chili, chopped finely
2 teaspoons olive oil
¼ cup finely chopped fresh dill
2lb 4oz piece skinless salmon fillet
1lb 2oz farfalle pasta
⅔ cup (160ml) dry white wine
2 tablespoons lemon juice
½ cup (125ml) cream
9oz baby rocket leaves

1 Preheat oven to 400°F.
2 Place onion, in single layer, in large baking dish with caperberries. Spray lightly with oil; roast, uncovered, about 25 minutes or until onion is softened.
3 Combine chili, oil and half the dill in small bowl. Place salmon on large baking-paper-lined oven tray; brush salmon both sides with chili mixture. Roast, uncovered, about 10 minutes or until salmon is just tender and cooked as desired.
4 Cook pasta in large pan of boiling water until tender.
5 Combine wine and juice in small pan; bring to the boil. Simmer, uncovered, about 5 minutes or until liquid reduces by half. Stir in cream and remaining dill.
6 Place drained pasta, flaked salmon, onion mixture and dill cream sauce in large bowl with rocket; toss gently.

prep & cook time 1 hour **serves** 8
nutritional count per serving 18.3g total fat (6.8g saturated fat); 520 cal; 49.6g carbohydrate; 33.7g protein; 3.8g fiber

All the flavors of the sunny south of France skyrocket in this salad. Rigatoni, a tube-shaped pasta with ridges on the outside, is ideal used in this salad: its wide hollow centre captures the dish's other ingredients and the dressing clings to the pasta's indentations. You can use black olive tapenade in this recipe, if you prefer.

warm pasta provençale salad

1lb 5oz lamb fillets

13oz rigatoni pasta

¾ cup (4oz) seeded black olives, halved

1 cup (5oz) drained semi-dried tomatoes in oil, chopped coarsely

14oz can artichoke hearts, drained, halved

1 small red onion (4oz), sliced thinly

2oz baby rocket leaves

½ cup (4oz) green olive tapenade

2 tablespoons olive oil

2 tablespoons lemon juice

1 Cook lamb in heated oiled large frying pan until cooked as desired. Cover; stand 5 minutes then slice thickly.
2 Meanwhile, cook pasta in large saucepan of boiling water until tender; drain.
3 Combine pasta with lamb and remaining ingredients in large bowl; serve warm.

prep & cook time 30 minutes **serves** 6
nutritional count per serving 16.9g total fat
(3.4g saturated fat); 527 cal; 57.4g carbohydrate;
32g protein; 7.5g fiber

pasta salad with green beans & tuna

13oz large pasta spirals
9oz green beans, trimmed, halved crossways
15oz canned tuna in oil
1 medium red pepper (7oz), sliced thinly
¾ cup loosely packed fresh flat-leaf parsley leaves
lemon dressing
2 cloves garlic, crushed
1 tablespoon finely grated lemon rind
1 teaspoon cracked black pepper
1 tablespoon lemon juice

1 Cook pasta in large saucepan of boiling water until tender; drain. Rinse under cold water; drain.
2 Meanwhile, boil, steam or microwave beans until just tender; drain. Rinse under cold water; drain.
3 Drain tuna over small bowl; reserve oil for dressing. Flake tuna into large chunks with fork.
4 Make lemon dressing.
5 Place pasta, beans and tuna in large bowl with dressing and remaining ingredients; toss gently.
lemon dressing Combine ingredients with reserved oil in screw-top jar; shake well.

prep & cook time 20 minutes **serves** 4
nutritional count per serving 26g total fat
(3.9g saturated fat); 658 cal; 67.5g carbohydrate;
35g protein; 6.2g fiber

gremolata lamb salad

9oz farfalle pasta

1lb 5oz asparagus, trimmed, halved crossways

7oz green beans, trimmed, halved crossways

1 tablespoon vegetable oil

1lb 13oz lamb fillets

2 teaspoons Dijon mustard

3 shallots (3oz), sliced thinly

⅓ cup (2oz) roasted pine nuts

⅓ cup loosely packed fresh flat-leaf parsley leaves

lemon dijon dressing

2 tablespoons lemon juice

2 tablespoons extra virgin olive oil

2 teaspoons Dijon mustard

gremolata

2 cloves garlic, chopped finely

1 tablespoon finely grated lemon rind

½ cup finely chopped fresh flat-leaf parsley

1 Make lemon Dijon dressing and gremolata.

2 Cook pasta in large saucepan of boiling water until tender; drain. Rinse under cold water; drain.

3 Meanwhile, boil, steam or microwave asparagus and beans, separately, until just tender; drain.

4 Heat oil in large frying pan; cook lamb, uncovered, until browned and cooked as desired. Spread mustard over lamb; press gremolata firmly onto mustard. Cover; stand 5 minutes. Slice lamb thickly.

5 Place pasta, asparagus, beans and lamb in large bowl with shallots, nuts, parsley and dressing; toss gently.

lemon dijon dressing Combine ingredients in screw-top jar; shake well.

gremolata Combine ingredients in small bowl.

prep & cook time 40 minutes **serves** 4
nutritional count per serving 41.2g total fat (10.5g saturated fat); 793 cal; 47.4g carbohydrate; 55g protein; 7.1g fiber

Farfalle is a bow-tie shaped short pasta sometimes known as butterfly or bow-tie pasta.

salmon pasta salad with lemon mayonnaise

9oz orecchiette pasta
20 caperberries (4oz), rinsed, drained
2 x 14oz cans red salmon, drained, flaked
1 large white onion (7oz), halved, sliced thinly
4 stalks celery (1lb 5oz), trimmed, sliced thinly
4 large red cabbage leaves, trimmed
lemon mayonnaise
2 tablespoons water
⅔ cup (7oz) mayonnaise
½ cup (4oz) sour cream
¼ cup (60ml) lemon juice
¼ cup coarsely chopped fresh dill

1 Cook pasta in large saucepan of boiling water until tender; drain. Rinse under cold water; drain.
2 Meanwhile, make lemon mayonnaise.
3 Slice eight caperberries thinly; combine in large bowl with salmon, onion, celery, pasta and half the mayonnaise; toss gently.
4 Divide cabbage among serving bowls; fill with salad, top with remaining mayonnaise and caperberries.
lemon mayonnaise Whisk ingredients in small bowl until well combined.

prep & cook time 25 minutes **serves** 4
nutritional count per serving 48.5g total fat (15.1g saturated fat); 871 cal; 60.6g carbohydrate; 45.7g protein; 6.1g fiber

Roasting the tomatoes concentrates the flavor, which goes well with pumpkin.
Serve the salad warm and accompany with a warm loaf of crusty bread.

pumpkin ravioli and roasted tomato salad

1lb 2oz cherry tomatoes, halved
2 medium red onions (12oz), halved, sliced thinly
1 teaspoon superfine sugar
¼ cup (60ml) olive oil
2lb 4oz pumpkin ravioli
4oz baby rocket leaves
5oz small black olives, seeded
2 tablespoons rinsed, drained baby capers
2 tablespoons red wine vinegar

1 Preheat oven to 425°F. Line oven tray with baking paper.
2 Place tomato and onion on tray in a single layer; sprinkle with sugar, drizzle with 1 tablespoon of the oil. Roast, uncovered, about 20 minutes.
3 Meanwhile, cook ravioli in large saucepan of boiling water until tender; drain, combine in large bowl with tomato, onion, rocket, olives and capers.
4 Drizzle salad with combined vinegar and remaining oil.

prep & cook time 30 minutes **serves** 6
nutritional count per serving 18g total fat
(4.7g saturated fat); 369 cal; 35g carbohydrate;
14.3g protein; 5.2g fiber

Instead of boiling the asparagus, break off the woody ends then halve the spears and cook them on a lightly oiled grill plate or under a grill until just tender and browned lightly. This recipe should be eaten while still warm, as the haloumi becomes tough and rubbery on cooling.

asparagus & grilled haloumi

9oz farfalle pasta
1lb 11oz asparagus, trimmed, chopped coarsely
9oz haloumi cheese, sliced thinly
1 medium avocado (9oz), sliced thinly
2 tablespoons coarsely chopped fresh chives
1 tablespoon finely grated lemon rind
¼ cup (60ml) lemon juice
⅓ cup (80ml) olive oil
1 teaspoon white sugar

1 Cook pasta in large saucepan of boiling water until tender; drain. Rinse under cold water; drain.
2 Meanwhile, boil, steam or microwave asparagus until just tender; drain well.
3 Cook haloumi, in batches, in medium frying pan until browned lightly; drain on absorbent paper.
4 Place pasta, asparagus and haloumi in large bowl with avocado, chives and combined remaining ingredients; toss gently.

prep & cook time 30 minutes **serves** 4
nutritional count per serving 39.6g total fat (11.7g saturated fat); 651 cal; 47.3g carbohydrate; 24.5g protein; 4.8g fiber

curried macaroni tuna & bean salad

9oz small macaroni pasta
7oz green beans, halved
7oz yellow string beans, halved
15oz can tuna in oil, drained, flaked
1 small red onion (3oz), sliced thinly
¼ cup finely chopped fresh flat-leaf parsley
½ cup (125ml) olive oil
¼ cup (60ml) lemon juice
2 cloves garlic, crushed
2 teaspoons curry powder

1   Cook pasta in large saucepan of boiling water until tender; drain. Rinse under cold water; drain.
2   Meanwhile, boil, steam or microwave beans until just tender; drain. Rinse under cold water; drain.
3   Place pasta and beans in large bowl with tuna, onion, parsley and combined remaining ingredients; toss gently.

prep & cook time 30 minutes **serves** 4
nutritional count per serving 41.1g total fat (6g saturated fat); 688 cal; 46.9g carbohydrate; 30.4g protein; 5.7g fiber

pasta salad with garlic vinaigrette

13oz penne pasta
7oz sun-dried tomatoes in oil
½ cup (3oz) roasted pine nuts, chopped coarsely
14oz bocconcini cheese, chopped coarsely
1 small red onion (4oz), sliced thinly
12 fresh purple basil leaves, torn
12 fresh basil leaves, torn
2 cloves garlic, crushed
1 tablespoon Dijon mustard
¼ cup (60ml) lemon juice

1 Cook pasta in large saucepan of boiling water until tender; drain. Rinse under cold water; drain.
2 Drain tomatoes; reserve oil. Slice tomatoes thickly.
3 Place pasta and tomato in large bowl with nuts, cheese, onion and both basils.
4 Combine reserved sun-dried tomato oil and remaining ingredients in screw-top jar; shake well. Drizzle over salad; toss gently.

prep & cook time 25 minutes **serves** 6
nutritional count per serving 21.8g total fat (7.6g saturated fat); 537 cal; 56.4g carbohydrate; 24.4g protein; 8.2g fiber

This recipe should be assembled just before serving. Purple basil, also known as opal basil, has an intense aroma and a longer shelf-life than sweet basil.

hot rigatoni salad with cauliflower

13oz rigatoni pasta
⅓ cup (80ml) olive oil
5 cloves garlic, chopped coarsely
1½ cups (4oz) stale breadcrumbs
13oz cauliflower florets
13oz broccoli florets
⅓ cup (80ml) lemon juice
1 cup coarsely chopped fresh flat-leaf parsley
½ cup (1oz) roasted flaked almonds

1 Cook pasta in large saucepan of boiling water until tender; drain. Rinse under cold water; drain.
2 Meanwhile, heat 2 tablespoons of the oil in large frying pan; cook garlic and breadcrumbs, stirring, until browned lightly. Place in large serving bowl.
3 Heat remaining oil in same pan; cook cauliflower and broccoli, in batches, stirring, until almost tender. Add vegetables to bowl with pasta, juice, parsley and nuts; toss gently.

prep & cook time 35 minutes **serves** 4
nutritional count per serving 26.3g total fat (3.3g saturated fat); 696 cal; 85.7g carbohydrate; 22.9g protein; 11.7g fiber

smoked salmon & dill salad

9oz linguine pasta
2 small fennel bulbs (14oz), trimmed, sliced thinly
1 medium red onion (6oz), sliced thinly
7oz smoked salmon, sliced thickly
¼ cup rinsed, drained capers, chopped coarsely
½ cup loosely packed fresh dill
½ cup (120ml) crème fraîche
2 teaspoons finely grated lemon rind
¼ cup (60ml) lemon juice

1 Cook pasta in large saucepan of boiling water until tender; drain. Rinse under cold water; drain.
2 Place pasta in large bowl with fennel, onion, salmon, capers, dill and combined remaining ingredients; toss gently to combine.

prep & cook time 25 minutes **serves** 4
nutritional count per serving 15.2g total fat (8.5g saturated fat); 425 cal; 49g carbohydrate; 20.5g protein; 4.4g fiber

The salad can be prepared several hours ahead; keep, covered, in the refrigerator. Pour over combined crème fraîche, rind and juice just before serving. You can replace the crème fraîche with sour cream, light sour cream or double cream if you prefer.

sweet chili shrimp pasta salad

9oz rigatoni pasta
2lb 4oz cooked large shrimp, shelled, tails intact
2 green onions, chopped finely
1 tablespoon coarsely chopped watercress
1 tablespoon coarsely chopped fresh coriander
½ Lebanese cucumber (5oz), chopped coarsely
½ cup (125ml) sweet chili sauce
1 teaspoon sesame oil
1 tablespoon lime juice

1 Cook pasta in large saucepan of boiling water until tender; drain. Rinse under cold water; drain.
2 Place pasta in large bowl with shrimp, onion, watercress, coriander, cucumber and combined remaining ingredients; toss gently to combine.

prep & cook time 20 minutes **serves** 4
nutritional count per serving 3.5g total fat (0.6g saturated fat); 376 cal; 59.8g carbohydrate; 33.3g protein; 4.1g fiber

spinach & prosciutto pasta salad

13oz large pasta spirals
12 slices prosciutto (6oz)
5oz baby spinach leaves
2 tablespoons wholegrain mustard
2 cloves garlic, crushed
½ cup (125ml) olive oil
¼ cup (60ml) lemon juice

1 Cook pasta in large saucepan of boiling water until tender; drain. Rinse under cold water; drain.
2 Meanwhile, cook prosciutto, in batches, in heated oiled large frying pan until browned and crisp; drain on absorbent paper, chop coarsely.
3 Place pasta and prosciutto in large bowl with spinach and combined remaining ingredients; toss gently.

prep & cook time 20 minutes **serves** 4
nutritional count per serving 32.4g total fat (5.2g saturated fat); 642 cal; 65.3g carbohydrate; 20.1g protein; 4.6g fiber

Finely slice or chop two hard-boiled eggs, if you wish, and toss them through this salad just before serving.

chicken, hazelnut & rocket salad

9oz linguine pasta
12oz chicken breast fillets
½ cup (3oz) hazelnuts, roasted, chopped coarsely
4oz curly endive
5oz baby rocket leaves
⅓ cup (80ml) lime juice
⅓ cup (80ml) olive oil
2 cloves garlic, crushed
2 teaspoons Dijon mustard

1 Cook pasta in large saucepan of boiling water until tender; drain. Rinse under cold water; drain.
2 Meanwhile, cook chicken on heated oiled grill plate (or grill or barbecue) until browned all over and cooked through. Stand 5 minutes; cut into thin slices.
3 Combine pasta and chicken in large bowl with nuts, endive, rocket and combined remaining ingredients; toss gently to combine.

prep & cook time 20 minutes **serves** 4
nutritional count per serving 34.8g total fat (4.6g saturated fat); 621 cal; 45g carbohydrate; 29.6g protein; 5.4g fiber

pasta caesar salad

7oz large pasta shells
5oz bacon, chopped finely
1 medium Romaine lettuce, torn
2 hard-boiled eggs, chopped coarsely
2 small avocados (14oz), chopped coarsely
½ cup (1oz) shaved Parmesan cheese
caesar dressing
1 egg
2 cloves garlic, quartered
2 tablespoons lemon juice
1 teaspoon Dijon mustard
8 drained anchovy fillets
¾ cup (180ml) olive oil

1 Cook pasta in large saucepan of boiling water until tender; drain. Rinse under cold water; drain.
2 Meanwhile, make Caesar dressing.
3 Cook bacon in small frying pan, stirring, until browned and crisp; drain on absorbent paper.
4 Place pasta and bacon in large bowl with lettuce, egg and avocado; pour over half the Caesar dressing, toss gently.
5 Divide salad among serving plates; drizzle with remaining dressing, sprinkle with cheese.
caesar dressing Blend or process egg, garlic, juice, mustard and anchovies until smooth. With motor operating, gradually add oil in a thin steady stream; process until dressing thickens.

prep & cook time 30 minutes **serves** 4
nutritional count per serving 70.1g total fat (14.3g saturated fat); 901 cal; 38.7g carbohydrate; 27.1g protein; 7.2g fiber

seafood pasta salad

1 teaspoon olive oil
1 small onion (3oz), sliced thinly
1 clove garlic, crushed
1lb 2oz seafood marinara mix
13oz large pasta shells
1 tablespoon dry white wine
½ cup (5oz) mayonnaise
1 teaspoon lemon juice
2 teaspoons Worcestershire sauce
⅓ cup (80ml) tomato sauce
¼ teaspoon Tabasco sauce
1 tablespoon coarsely chopped fresh flat-leaf parsley
4oz baby rocket leaves

1 Heat oil in large frying pan; cook onion and garlic, stirring, until onion softens. Add marinara mix; cook, stirring, about 5 minutes or until seafood is cooked through. Place marinara mixture in large bowl, cover; refrigerate until cold.
2 Cook pasta in large saucepan of boiling water until tender; drain. Rinse under cold water; drain.
3 Place pasta and combined wine, mayonnaise, juice, sauces and parsley in bowl with marinara mixture; toss gently. Serve seafood salad on rocket leaves.

prep & cook time 25 minutes (+ refrigeration) **serves** 4
nutritional count per serving 18.2g total fat
(2.7g saturated fat); 672 cal; 80.1g carbohydrate;
42.9g protein; 4.5g fiber

roasted pepper, goat cheese & walnut salad

13oz large spiral pasta
2 medium red peppers (14oz)
2 medium yellow peppers (14oz)
5oz goat cheese, crumbled
⅓ cup (1oz) walnuts, roasted, chopped coarsely
½ cup loosely packed fresh basil leaves
¼ cup (60ml) red wine vinegar
⅓ cup (80ml) olive oil
1 clove garlic, crushed
2 teaspoons wholegrain mustard

1 Cook pasta in large saucepan of boiling water until tender; drain. Rinse under cold water; drain.
2 Meanwhile, quarter peppers; discard seeds and membranes. Roast, skin-side up, under very hot grill until skin blisters and blackens. Cover pepper in plastic or paper for 5 minutes; peel away skin then slice pepper thickly.
3 Place pasta and pepper in large bowl with cheese, nuts, basil and combined vinegar, oil, garlic and mustard; toss gently.

prep & cook time 30 minutes **serves** 4
nutritional count per serving 31.5g total fat (7g saturated fat); 655 cal; 70.4g carbohydrate; 23.8g protein; 5.7g fiber

Feta or any soft, crumbly cheese can be substituted for the goat cheese, and roasted pecan halves can be used instead of the walnuts.

You need two bunches of fresh coriander, including the roots and stems as well as the leaves.

lamb & pasta with walnut coriander pesto

13oz farfalle pasta
4 lamb fillets (14oz)
1½ cups firmly packed, coarsely chopped
    fresh coriander (*see note, above*)
½ cup (2oz) walnuts, roasted
½ cup (1oz) coarsely grated Parmesan cheese
2 cloves garlic, quartered
½ cup (125ml) light olive oil
1 tablespoon drained preserved lemon, chopped finely
½ cup (5oz) yogurt
2 teaspoons light olive oil, extra
2 teaspoons lemon juice

1 Cook pasta in large saucepan of boiling water until tender; drain. Rinse under cold water; drain.
2 Meanwhile, cook lamb in heated oiled large frying pan until cooked as desired. Cover lamb; stand for 5 minutes then slice thinly.
3 Reserve 2 tablespoons of coriander leaves. Blend or process remaining coriander, nuts, cheese, garlic and oil until mixture forms a smooth paste. Combine mixture with pasta in large bowl.
4 Divide pasta among serving plates, top with lamb and preserved lemon; drizzle with combined yogurt, extra oil and juice, then top with reserved coriander leaves.

prep & cook time 25 minutes **serves** 4
nutritional count per serving 48.5g total fat (9.5g saturated fat); 867 cal; 66.8g carbohydrate; 38.9g protein; 4.9g fiber

bacon and corn pasta salad with mustard dressing

1lb 2oz pasta
1 tablespoon olive oil
9oz button mushrooms, halved
9oz bacon, chopped coarsely
8oz baby corn
1 medium red onion (6oz), chopped coarsely
1 large avocado (11oz), chopped coarsely
1 cup fresh flat-leaf parsley leaves
mustard dressing
1 cup (250ml) bottled Caesar salad dressing
1 tablespoon wholegrain mustard

1 Cook pasta in large saucepan of boiling water until tender; drain. Rinse under cold water; drain.
2 Meanwhile, heat oil in large frying pan, add mushrooms and bacon; cook, stirring, until beginning to brown. Remove mixture from pan. Add corn to same pan; cook, stirring, until browned lightly all over.
3 Make mustard dressing.
4 Place pasta, mushroom mixture and corn in large bowl with onion, avocado, parsley and dressing; toss gently.
mustard dressing Combine ingredients in small bowl.

prep & cook time 30 minutes **serves** 6
nutritional count per serving 39.4g total fat
(6g saturated fat); 704 cal; 65.2g carbohydrate;
19.2g protein; 7g fiber

warm salami and tomato pasta salad

13oz orecchiette pasta

7oz thinly sliced hot salami

⅓ cup (2oz) roasted pine nuts, chopped coarsely

9oz cherry tomatoes

9oz grape tomatoes, halved

⅓ cup fresh flat-leaf parsley leaves

⅓ cup torn fresh basil leaves

¼ cup (1oz) shaved pecorino cheese

red wine vinegar dressing

⅓ cup (80ml) olive oil

¼ cup (60ml) red wine vinegar

2 cloves garlic, crushed

1 Cook pasta in large saucepan of boiling water until tender; drain. Rinse under cold water; drain.

2 Meanwhile, cook salami in large frying pan, stirring, until crisp; drain on absorbent paper.

3 Make red wine vinegar dressing.

4 Place pasta, dressing, salami, nuts, tomatoes, herbs and cheese in large bowl; toss gently.

red wine vinegar dressing Place ingredients in screw-top jar; shake well.

prep & cook time 25 minutes **serves** 4

nutritional count per serving 50.1g total fat (10.4 saturated fat); 836 cal; 68.2g carbohydrate; 25.6g protein; 6.4g fiber

Use any variety of ravioli you like so long as the filling does not include any meat.

You can use any kind of prepared pesto in this salad's dressing – roasted vegetable pesto is also good.

You need approximately 1lb 2oz untrimmed broccoli to get the amount of florets needed for this recipe.

ravioli salad

13oz packaged spinach and ricotta ravioli
9oz bacon, chopped coarsely
3 cups (9oz) broccoli florets
9oz cherry tomatoes, halved
2 tablespoons finely sliced fresh basil
½ cup (125ml) olive oil
¼ cup (60ml) white wine vinegar
2 tablespoons sun-dried tomato pesto

1 Cook pasta in large saucepan of boiling water until pasta floats to the top. Rinse under cold water; drain.
2 Meanwhile, cook bacon in small frying pan, stirring, until browned and crisp; drain on absorbent paper.
3 Boil, steam or microwave broccoli until just tender, drain. Rinse under cold water; drain.
4 Place pasta, bacon and broccoli in large bowl with tomato, basil and combined remaining ingredients; toss gently.

prep & cook time 30 minutes **serves** 4
nutritional count per serving 45.9g total fat (9.9g saturated fat); 573 cal; 15.1g carbohydrate; 23.8g protein; 5.2g fiber

chickpea, preserved lemon and risoni salad

9oz frozen peas

1¼ cups (10oz) risoni

1 tablespoon olive oil

2 cloves garlic, crushed

1 celery stalk (5oz), trimmed, chopped finely

14oz can chickpeas, rinsed, drained

2 pieces preserved lemon (3oz), trimmed,
    chopped finely

⅓ cup (2oz) seeded black olives

4oz goat cheese, crumbled

yogurt dressing

⅓ cup (3oz) greek-style yogurt

1 tablespoon white wine vinegar

1 Boil, steam or microwave peas until tender.

2 Meanwhile, make yogurt dressing.

3 Cook risoni in medium saucepan of boiling water until tender; drain.

4 Meanwhile, heat oil in large frying pan; cook garlic and celery, stirring, until celery softens slightly. Stir in chickpeas, lemon, olives, risoni and peas. Sprinkle cheese over salad; drizzle with dressing.

yogurt dressing Place ingredients in small bowl; whisk until combined.

prep & cook time 35 minutes **serves** 4
nutritional count per serving 13.4g total fat
(5.1g saturated fat); 491 cal; 66g carbohydrate;
21g protein; 10.4g fiber

Preserved lemons are a North African specialty; lemons are quartered and preserved in salt and lemon juice or water. To use, remove and discard pulp, squeeze juice from rind, rinse rind well then slice thinly. Sold in Middle-Eastern food shops, major supermarkets and delicatessens.

warm gnocchi salad

7oz jar char-grilled peppers in oil
2 tablespoons red wine vinegar
2 cloves garlic, crushed
⅓ cup (80ml) olive oil
1lb 2oz potato gnocchi
½ cup (3oz) black olives
12oz jar marinated artichoke hearts, drained, quartered
1 medium red onion (5oz), sliced thinly
½ cup firmly packed fresh basil leaves
⅓ cup (1oz) roasted walnuts

1 Drain peppers, reserve oil (you will need ¼ cup oil). Slice peppers thinly.
2 Combine reserved pepper oil with vinegar, garlic and olive oil in screw-top jar; shake well.
3 Cook gnocchi in large saucepan of boiling water until gnocchi float to the surface; drain.
4 Combine pepper, olives, artichokes, onion, basil and gnocchi in large bowl; add oil mixture. Sprinkle with nuts.

prep & cook time 15 minutes **serves** 4
nutritional count per serving 41.4g total fat (5.5g saturated fat); 602 cal; 44.8g carbohydrate; 9.9g protein; 5.6g fiber

chili tuna pasta salad

11oz large pasta shells
9oz green beans, trimmed, halved
2 x 7oz cans tuna in chili oil
⅓ cup coarsely chopped fresh flat-leaf parsley
⅓ cup firmly packed fresh basil leaves, torn
2 tablespoons rinsed, drained baby capers
5oz baby rocket leaves
¼ cup (60ml) olive oil
¼ cup (60ml) lemon juice
2 cloves garlic, crushed
2 teaspoons white sugar

1 Cook pasta in large saucepan of boiling water until tender; drain. Rinse under cold water; drain.
2 Meanwhile, boil, steam or microwave beans until just tender; drain. Rinse under cold water; drain.
3 Drain tuna; reserve oil. Place tuna in large bowl; flake with fork. Add pasta, beans, herbs, capers and rocket to bowl; toss gently.
4 Place remaining ingredients and reserved oil in screw-top jar; shake well. Drizzle over salad; toss gently.

prep & cook time 30 minutes **serves** 6
nutritional count per serving 16.8g total fat (2.5g saturated fat); 389 cal; 37.9g carbohydrate; 19.6g protein; 3.6g fiber

You can use any short pasta you like instead of the spirals. The vegetables used in this recipe are available from most delicatessens, or bottled from supermarkets.

deli pasta salad

1lb 2oz large spiral pasta
5oz drained char-grilled eggplant, chopped coarsely
5oz drained char-grilled pepper, chopped coarsely
5oz semi-dried tomatoes
5oz sliced salami, cut into strips
⅓ cup small fresh basil leaves
pesto dressing
1 cup (250ml) bottled Italian dressing
2 tablespoons basil pesto

1 Cook pasta in large saucepan of boiling water until tender; drain. Rinse under cold water; drain.
2 Meanwhile, make pesto dressing.
3 Place pasta and dressing in large bowl with remaining ingredients; toss gently.
pesto dressing Combine ingredients in screw-top jar; shake well.

prep & cook time 20 minutes **serves** 6
nutritional count per serving 29.1g total fat (5.9g saturated fat); 636 cal; 70.6g carbohydrate; 19g protein; 7.8g fiber

sesame beef and pasta salad

1lb 2oz spaghettini pasta
2lb 4oz beef rump steak, sliced thinly
1 clove garlic, crushed
2 tablespoons sweet chili sauce
1 tablespoon peanut oil
1 medium yellow pepper (7oz), sliced thinly
1 medium carrot (4oz), sliced thickly
4oz trimmed watercress
5oz snow peas, trimmed, sliced thinly
2 teaspoons sesame seeds, toasted
sesame dressing
⅓ cup (80ml) peanut oil
½ teaspoon sesame oil
⅓ cup (80ml) rice vinegar
2 tablespoons light soy sauce
1 tablespoon lemon juice
1 green onion, sliced thinly

1 Cook pasta in large saucepan of boiling water until tender; drain. Rinse under cold water; drain.
2 Meanwhile, combine beef, garlic and sauce in large bowl. Heat oil in wok; stir-fry beef mixture, in batches, until beef is cooked as desired. Remove from pan.
3 Make sesame dressing.
4 Place pasta, beef mixture and dressing in large bowl with vegetables; toss gently. Sprinkle with sesame seeds.
sesame dressing Combine ingredients in screw-top jar; shake well.

prep & cook time 35 minutes **serves** 6
nutritional count per serving 22.1g total fat
(5g saturated fat); 664 cal; 61.8g carbohydrate;
51g protein; 5.3g fiber

bucatini & casarecci

Casarecci is made from rolled, twisted tubes of pasta, whereas bucatini is a long, hollow pasta; it looks a bit like thick spaghetti, but has a tube running down the centre. Both go well with chunkier-style sauces.

bucatini with pancetta and tomatoes

9oz bucatini pasta
2 tablespoons olive oil
2 medium onions (11oz), chopped finely
9oz pancetta, chopped coarsely
2 x 15oz cans whole tomatoes, drained, chopped
4 bocconcini cheese (5oz), torn
1 tablespoon fresh flat-leaf parsley leaves

1 Cook pasta in large pan of boiling water until tender; drain.
2 Meanwhile, heat oil in large saucepan; cook onion and pancetta, stirring, until onion is soft. Add tomatoes; cook, stirring, 2 minutes. Stir in pasta until heated through. Top with cheese and parsley.

prep & cook time 25 minutes **serves** 4
nutritional count per serving 24.1g total fat (8.2g saturated fat); 556 cal; 53.7g carbohydrate; 27.9g protein; 6g fiber

bucatini with moroccan lamb sauce

2 teaspoons olive oil
1 small onion (3oz), chopped finely
2 cloves garlic, crushed
1lb 2oz ground lamb
1 teaspoon ground cumin
½ teaspoon cayenne pepper
½ teaspoon ground cinnamon
2 tablespoons tomato paste
2 x 14oz cans crushed tomatoes
1 large zucchini (5oz), chopped coarsely
2 tablespoons finely chopped fresh mint
13oz bucatini pasta

1 Heat oil in large saucepan; cook onion and garlic, stirring, until onion softens. Add lamb; cook, stirring, until changed in color. Add spices; cook, stirring, until fragrant.
2 Stir in paste, undrained tomatoes and zucchini; bring to the boil. Reduce heat, simmer, uncovered, about 15 minutes or until sauce thickens slightly. Stir in mint.
3 Meanwhile, cook pasta in large saucepan of boiling water until tender; drain. Serve pasta topped with sauce.

prep & cook time 30 minutes **serves** 4
nutritional count per serving 14.9g total fat (5.5g saturated fat); 603 cal; 73.2g carbohydrate; 39.5g protein; 7.2g fiber

Baked ricotta is available from most supermarkets, delicatessens and specialty cheese shops. It is a baked fresh ricotta cheese; egg whites, paprika and oil are often added.

bucatini with baked ricotta

13oz bucatini pasta
2 x 10oz jars marinated eggplant in oil
2 cloves garlic, crushed
2 x 14oz cans crushed tomatoes
½ teaspoon cracked black pepper
11oz baked ricotta cheese, chopped coarsely

1 Cook pasta in large saucepan of boiling water until tender; drain.
2 Meanwhile, cook undrained eggplant and garlic in large saucepan, stirring, until fragrant.
3 Add pasta to eggplant mixture with undrained tomatoes and pepper; toss over medium heat until combined. Gently stir in cheese.

prep & cook time 20 minutes **serves** 4
nutritional count per serving 16.7g total fat (7.3g saturated fat); 547 cal; 73.6g carbohydrate; 21.1g protein; 7.9g fiber

chicken, chorizo and pepper with casarecci

⅓ cup (80ml) extra virgin olive oil
2 chorizo sausages (11oz), sliced thinly
1 medium red pepper (7oz), sliced thinly
14oz chicken breast fillets, sliced thinly
13oz casarecci pasta
2 cloves garlic, crushed
½ cup (2oz) green olives
½ cup coarsely chopped fresh flat-leaf parsley

1 Heat one tablespoon of the oil in large frying pan; cook chorizo and pepper, stirring, until pepper softens. Remove from pan.
2 Add chicken, in batches, to same pan; cook, stirring, until chicken is browned and cooked through. Return chorizo mixture to pan with chicken.
3 Meanwhile, cook pasta in large saucepan of boiling water until tender; drain.
4 Add garlic and olives to chicken mixture; cook, stirring, 2 minutes. Toss chicken mixture with remaining oil, parsley and pasta.

prep & cook time 30 minutes **serves** 4
nutritional count per serving 46.2g total fat
(12.2g saturated fat); 869 cal; 69.5g carbohydrate;
41.8g protein; 4.6g fiber

bucatini puttanesca with tuna

16oz can tuna
¼ cup chili oil
2 cloves garlic, crushed
4 drained anchovies, chopped
¼ teaspoon dried chili flakes
1½ cups (375ml) bottled tomato pasta sauce
1lb 2oz bucatini pasta
½ cup (3oz) black olives
2 tablespoons rinsed, drained baby capers
fresh basil leaves, for serving

1   Drain tuna over bowl. Using fork, flake tuna into bite-sized pieces.
2   Heat oil in large saucepan; cook garlic, anchovies and chilies, stirring, until fragrant. Add tuna and sauce to pan; simmer until thickened slightly.
3   Meanwhile, cook pasta in large saucepan of boiling water until tender. Drain pasta, reserving ⅓ cup pasta cooking liquid; return pasta to pan.
4   Combine pasta with tuna mixture, reserved cooking liquid, olives and capers; sprinkle with basil leaves.

prep & cook time 20 minutes **serves** 4
nutritional count per serving 28.7g total fat
(4.2g saturated fat); 825 cal; 99.5g carbohydrate;
38.5g protein; 6.6g fiber

casarecci with spring greens and goat cheese

14oz frozen broad beans
1lb 2oz casarecci pasta
⅓ cup (80ml) olive oil
2 small zucchini (6oz), sliced thinly
1 clove garlic, crushed
5oz shelled fresh peas
5oz goat cheese, crumbled
½ cup loosely packed fresh mint leaves
lemon and garlic crumbs
1oz butter
1 tablespoon olive oil
1 clove garlic, crushed
1 teaspoon finely grated lemon rind
1 cup (3oz) coarse fresh breadcrumbs

1 Place broad beans in large heatproof bowl, cover with boiling water; stand 10 minutes. Drain. When cool enough to handle, peel gray outer shells from beans; discard shells.
2 Meanwhile, cook pasta in large saucepan of boiling water until tender; drain. Return pasta to pan, cover to keep warm.
3 Heat oil in large saucepan, add zucchini, garlic and peas; cook, stirring, about 5 minutes or until zucchini is softened. Add broad beans, cook 1 minute.
4 Make lemon and garlic crumbs.
5 Combine pasta with zucchini mixture, cheese and mint leaves. Top with lemon and garlic crumbs to serve.
lemon and garlic crumbs Heat butter and oil in medium frying pan, add garlic, rind and breadcrumbs; cook, stirring, until breadcrumbs are golden and crisp.

prep & cook time 35 minutes **serves** 4
nutritional count per serving 39.6g total fat (12.9g saturated fat); 953 cal; 110.8g carbohydrate; 29.8g protein; 16.7g fiber

We've used casarecci, short lengths of rolled and twisted pasta, but you can use any short pasta such as penne or rigatoni. You could use leftover roast squash in this recipe; reheat it in the microwave oven, then add it to the pasta as per step 3.

creamy squash, artichoke and prosciutto pasta

3lb 6oz butternut squash, cut into ½in pieces
1lb 2oz casarecci pasta
2 tablespoons olive oil
12 slices prosciutto (6oz), chopped coarsely
1¼ cups (300ml) cream
11oz drained marinated artichoke hearts,
    cut into thin wedges
7oz baby spinach leaves
¾ cup firmly packed fresh flat-leaf parsley leaves
⅓ cup (1oz) finely grated Parmesan cheese

1 Boil, steam or microwave squash until tender. Drain, cover to keep warm.
2 Meanwhile, cook pasta in large saucepan of boiling water until tender. Drain pasta, reserving ⅓ cup of the cooking liquid.
3 Heat oil in same pan; cook prosciutto, stirring, until crisp. Add cream and reserved cooking liquid to pan; bring to the boil. Reduce heat, gently stir in squash, pasta and artichoke; simmer until heated through. Remove from heat; stir in spinach and parsley. Serve sprinkled with cheese.

prep & cook time 30 minutes **serves** 6
nutritional count per serving 33g total fat
(17.6g saturated fat); 712 cal; 75.2g carbohydrate;
24.5g protein; 8.4g fiber

glossary

ARTICHOKE HEARTS tender center of the globe artichoke. Purchase fresh, or in oil or brine in glass jars.

BEANS

broad also known as fava or Windsor beans; available dried, fresh, canned or frozen. Fresh or frozen are best peeled twice, discarding both the outer long green pod and the beige-green tough inner shell.

kidney medium-sized red bean, slightly floury in texture yet sweet in flavor.

sprouts tender new growths of assorted beans and seeds germinated for consumption. The most readily available are mung beans, soya beans, alfalfa and snow pea sprouts.

BOK CHOY also known as pak choi, Chinese white cabbage and Chinese chard, has a mild mustard taste. Baby bok choy is smaller and more tender.

CAPERBERRIES fruit formed after the caper buds have flowered; they are pickled, usually with stalks intact.

CAPERS the gray-green buds of a warm climate shrub, sold either dried and salted or pickled in a vinegar brine.

CHEESE

brie smooth and rich, brie has a bloomy white rind and a creamy center that becomes runnier as it ripens.

feta a white cheese with milky, fresh acidity. Most commonly made from cow's milk, though sheep and goat's milk varieties are available. Feta is matured in brine for at least a month, which imparts a strong salty flavor. Feta is solid but crumbles readily.

goat cheese made from goat's milk, has an earthy, strong taste; available in both soft and firm textures, and is sometimes rolled in ash or herbs.

gorgonzola originally from the Lombardy region of Italy; a creamy, cow's-milk blue-moulded cheese.

haloumi a firm, cream-colored sheep-milk cheese matured in brine; like a salty feta in flavor. Should be eaten while still warm as it becomes tough on cooling.

mascarpone a cultured cream product. Whitish to creamy yellow in color, it has a soft, creamy texture, a high fat content and a fresh tangy taste.

mozzarella a semi-soft cheese with a delicate, fresh taste; has a low melting point and stringy texture when hot.

Parmesan also known as parmigiano, is a hard, grainy cheese. The curd is salted in brine for a month before being aged for up to two years in humid conditions.

pecorino the generic Italian name for cheeses made from sheep milk. It's a hard, white to pale yellow cheese. Use Parmesan, if unavailable.

pizza cheese a blend of grated mozzarella, cheddar and Parmesan cheeses.

ricotta a sweet, fairly moist, fresh curd cheese having a low fat content.

CHILIES available in many types and sizes. Wear rubber gloves to seed and chop fresh chilies as they can burn your skin. Removing membranes and seeds lessens the heat level.

cayenne pepper a thin-fleshed, long, extremely hot red chili; usually purchased dried and ground.

flakes crushed dried red chilies.

red Thai small, medium hot and bright red in color.

CHINESE COOKING WINE also known as hao hsing or Chinese rice wine; made from fermented rice, wheat, sugar and salt with a 13.5 percent alcohol content. Inexpensive and found in Asian food shops; if you can't find it, replace with mirin or sherry.

CHORIZO a sausage of Spanish origin, made from coarsely ground pork and highly seasoned with garlic and chili.

COCONUT CREAM the first pressing from grated mature coconut flesh; available in cans and cartons.

CORIANDER also known as cilantro or Chinese parsley; bright-green leafy herb with a pungent flavor; the whole plant (roots, stems and leaves) is used in Asian cooking. Also sold as seeds, whole or ground, however, these cannot be used in place of the fresh herb as the tastes are completely different.

CRÈME FRAÎCHE (minimum fat content 35%) a mature fermented cream having a slightly tangy, nutty flavor and velvety texture. Available from supermarkets.

CURRY POWDER a blend of ground spices used for convenience when making Indian food. Choose mild or hot to suit your taste.

ENDIVE, CURLY also known as frisée; a curly-leafed green vegetable, mainly used in salads.

FENNEL a white to very pale green-white, firm, crisp, roundish vegetable about 8-12cm in diameter. The bulb has a slightly sweet, anise flavor but the leaves have a much stronger taste. Also the name given to dried seeds having a licorice flavor.

FISH SAUCE also called nam pla or nuoc nam; made from pulverized salted fermented fish, usually anchovies. Has a pungent smell and strong taste, so use according to your taste.

FIVE-SPICE POWDER a fragrant mix of ground cinnamon, cloves, star anise, Sichuan pepper and fennel seeds. Also known as Chinese five-spice.

FLAT-LEAF PARSLEY also known as continental parsley or Italian parsley.

GALANGAL also known as laos. It looks like ginger but is more dense and fibrous and much harder to cut. Adds a distinctive peppery flavor to food. Fresh ginger can be substituted for galangal, but the flavor will not be the same.

GINGER also known as green or root ginger; the thick gnarled root of a tropical plant. Cannot be substituted for powdered ginger.

pickled can be either pink or red colored and is available from Asian food shops. The paper-thin shavings of ginger are pickled in a mixture of vinegar, sugar and natural food coloring.

GNOCCHI Italian dumplings made of potatoes, semolina or flour.

GOW GEE WRAPPERS pastry sheets made of flour, egg and water; found in the refrigerated or freezer section of Asian food shops and many supermarkets. Wonton wrappers, spring roll or egg pastry sheets can be substituted.

HAZELNUTS also known as filberts; plump, grape-sized nuts having a brown inedible skin removed by rubbing heated nuts together vigorously in a tea-towel.

HERBS we have specified when to use fresh or dried herbs. We used dried (not ground) herbs in the proportion of 1:4 for fresh herbs; use 1 teaspoon dried herbs instead of 4 teaspoons (1 tablespoon) chopped fresh herbs.

KAFFIR LIME LEAVES also known as bai magrood, look like they are two glossy dark green leaves joined end to end, forming a rounded hourglass shape; used fresh or dried. A strip of fresh lime peel may be substituted for each kaffir lime leaf.

KALAMATA OLIVES small, sharp-tasting, brine-cured black olives.

LAKSA PASTE a bottled paste of lemon grass, chilies, galangal, shrimp paste, onions and turmeric. Commercial laksa pastes vary dramatically in their heat intensity so adjust the amount to suit your heat tolerance.

LEMON GRASS a tall, clumping, lemon-smelling and tasting, sharp-edged grass; the white lower part of each stem is often chopped finely when used in cooking.

MUSHROOMS
flat large, flat mushrooms with a rich earthy flavor. They are sometimes misnamed field mushrooms, which are wild mushrooms.
Swiss brown also known as cremini or roman mushrooms, are light brown mushrooms having a full-bodied flavor. Button mushrooms can be substituted.

OIL
olive made from ripened olives. Extra virgin and virgin are the best, while extra light or light refers to taste rather than fat levels.
peanut pressed from ground peanuts; most commonly used oil in Asian cooking because of its high smoke point (ability to reach high temperatures without burning).
sesame made from roasted, crushed sesame seeds. Used mainly as a flavoring.

PALM SUGAR also known as nam tan pip, jaggery, jawa or gula melaka; made from the sap of the sugar palm tree. Usually sold in rock-hard cakes; substitute it with brown sugar, if unavailable.

PAPRIKA ground dried red pepper, available sweet, hot or smoked.

PESTO a paste originally made from basil, oil, garlic, pine nuts and Parmesan. These days, bottled versions, made from such ingredients as sun-dried tomatoes and peppers, roasted vegetables and coriander are available from major supermarkets and deilcatessens.

PINE NUTS also known as pignoli; small, cream-colored kernels from the cones of different varieties of pine trees.

PINK PEPPERCORNS not true peppercorns but actually the dried berry from a type of rose plant grown in Madagascar; usually sold packed in brine (occasionally found freeze-dried). They possess a distinctive pungently sweet taste that goes well with cream sauces.

PISTACHIO a pale green, delicately flavored nut found inside a hard off-white shell. To peel, soak shelled nuts in boiling water for 5 minutes; drain, then pat dry with absorbent paper. Rub skins with a cloth to peel.

PRESERVED LEMONS a North African specialty; lemons are quartered and preserved in salt and lemon juice. To use, remove and discard pulp, squeeze juice from rind, rinse rind well; slice thinly. Sold in Middle-Eastern food shops, major supermarkets and delicatessens.

PROSCIUTTO a kind of unsmoked Italian ham; salted, air-cured and aged, it is usually eaten uncooked.

ROCKET also known as arugula, rugula and rucola; a peppery-tasting green leaf. Baby rocket, also known as wild rocket, is both smaller and less peppery.

SAFFRON stigma of a member of the crocus family, available in strands or ground form; imparts a yellow-orange color to food once infused in hot water. Very expensive, it should be stored in the freezer.

SAMBAL OELEK (also ulek or olek) Indonesian in origin; a salty paste made from ground chilies.

SEAFOOD MARINARA MIX a mixture of uncooked chopped seafood available from fish markets and fishmongers.

SNOW PEAS also called mange tout ('eat all'). A small fresh pea that can be eaten whole, pod and all.

STAR ANISE a dried star-shaped fruit of a tree native to China. The pods, which have an astringent aniseed or licorice flavor, are widely used in the Asian kitchen. Available whole or ground.

SWEET CHILI SAUCE a comparatively mild, Thai-style sauce made from red chilies, sugar, garlic and vinegar.

TOMATOES
semi-dried partially dried tomato pieces in olive oil. Softer and juicier than sun-dried, these are not preserves so do not keep as long as sun-dried. Usually sold marinated in herbed olive oil; they are soft enough to be consumed without needing to be reconstituted.
sun-dried totally dehydrated tomatoes sold bottled in oil or packaged in plastic; they need to be reconstituted before being eaten. We used sun-dried tomatoes in oil, unless otherwise specified.

VINEGAR
balsamic authentic only from the province of Modena, Italy; aged in antique wooden casks to give the exquisite pungent taste. It is a deep rich brown color with a sweet and sour flavor.
rice a colorless vinegar made from fermented rice and flavored with sugar and salt. It is also available as seasoned rice vinegar.
sherry made from a blend of wines and left in wood vats to mature where they develop a rich mellow flavor.

WOMBOK also known as Peking cabbage, Chinese cabbage or petsai. Elongated in shape with pale green, crinkly leaves, this is the most common cabbage in South-East Asian cooking.

WONTON WRAPPERS see gow gee wrappers.

WORCESTERSHIRE SAUCE a thin, dark-brown spicy sauce that is used both as a seasoning and condiment.

ZUCCHINI also known as courgette; small, pale- or dark-green, yellow or white vegetable belonging to the squash family. When young, its edible flowers can be stuffed then deep-fried or oven-baked.

conversion chart

MEASURES

The difference between one country's measuring cups and another's is, at most, within a 2 or 3 teaspoon variance, and will not affect your cooking results.

All cup and spoon measurements are level. The most accurate way of measuring dry ingredients is to weigh them. When measuring liquids, use a clear glass or plastic jug with graduated markings.

We use large eggs with an average weight of 2oz.

DRY MEASURES

IMPERIAL	METRIC
½oz	15g
1oz	30g
2oz	60g
3oz	90g
4oz (¼lb)	125g
5oz	155g
6oz	185g
7oz	220g
8oz (½lb)	250g
9oz	280g
10oz	315g
11oz	345g
12oz (¾lb)	375g
13oz	410g
14oz	440g
15oz	470g
16oz (1lb)	500g
24oz (1½lb)	750g
32oz (2lb)	1kg

LIQUID MEASURES

IMPERIAL	METRIC
1 fluid oz	30ml
2 fluid oz	60ml
3 fluid oz	100ml
4 fluid oz	125ml
5 fluid oz (¼ pint/1 gill)	150ml
6 fluid oz	190ml
8 fluid oz	250ml
16 fluid oz (1 pint)	500ml
1 quart	1000ml (1 litre)

LENGTH MEASURES

IMPERIAL	METRIC
⅛in	3mm
¼in	6mm
½in	1cm
¾in	2cm
1in	2.5cm
2in	5cm
2½in	6cm
3in	8cm
4in	10cm
5in	13cm
6in	15cm
7in	18cm
8in	20cm
9in	23cm
10in	25cm
11in	28cm
12in (1ft)	30cm

OVEN TEMPERATURES

These oven temperatures are only a guide for conventional ovens. For fan-forced ovens, check the manufacturer's manual.

	°C (CELSIUS)	°F (FAHRENHEIT)
Very slow	120	250
Slow	150	275-300
Moderately slow	160	325
Moderate	180	350-375
Moderately hot	200	400
Hot	220	425-450
Very hot	240	475

index